THE INTERNET WRITER'S
HANDBOOK 2001/2

a&b

THE INTERNET WRITER'S HANDBOOK 2001/2

Karen Scott

First published in Great Britain in 2001 by
ALLISON & BUSBY Limited
Suite 111, Bon Marche Centre
241-251 Ferndale Road
Brixton, London SW9 8BJ
http://www.allisonandbusby.ltd.uk

A catalogue record for this book is available from the British Library

ISBN 0 7490 04915

Printed and bound in Spain by
Liberdúplex, s. l. Barcelona

CONTENTS

INTRODUCTION   9

1   EZINES   10
What are ezines?   10
How to assess a website   13
Basic guidelines for submission   15
The markets [an A-Z listing]   23
Who wants what?   113
Who pays what?   120
Payment Chart   125

2   E-BOOKS PUBLISHING   130
What is an e-book?   130
How do I read an e-book?   131
Why e-publish?   136
E-book publishers [an A-Z listing]   142
Quick guide to royalty payments   220

3   OTHER INFORMATION   226
Copyright and contract   226
E-book Rights   233
Search methods   234
Resources for freelance writers   254
Competitions   257
Where is it all going?   264

GLOSSARY OF TERMS   271
INDEX   281

INTRODUCTION

The Internet Writer's Handbook 2001 offers a comprehensive guide to some of the best paying markets for writers on the internet set out in a user friendly A-Z format. It covers fiction and non-fiction, ezines, online magazines and e-book sites, and within these categories you will find information about submitting poetry, short stories, articles, and complete novels or non-fiction manuscripts across a wide variety of categories. It will provide you with the information you need to submit material to these websites by giving detailed listings under the website headings on submission guidelines, contact details, payment available and much more. It will provide you with an additional assessment facility by listing a number of websites according to market potential that I consider to be the best in their category.

The handbook also considers some broader issues, such as how to write for the internet user, search methods, how to assess a website and the information found on that site, and looks at new opportunities available to writers via the internet. It briefly discusses the impact of copyright and looks at points to consider when signing electronic rights contracts.

The e-book has been pushed to the forefront of technology on the internet with the introduction of Microsoft Reader, Rocket eBook/SoftBook and Glassbook, and other emerging technologies, and every writer needs to familiarise themselves with the opportunities available to them via this technology. The handbook will describe how e-books work, what potential lies in publishing this way, and the impact this may have on the future of publishing and writing in general.

The handbook also takes in the basics, by providing you with an overview of submission guidelines you might expect to find on the internet and what they mean, what search methods to use and how to assess the material you find.

1

EZINES

What are ezines?

Ezines are electronic publications, and are variously known as electronic magazines, zines, webzines, fanzines or mags. They are always available online and are publicly accessible, usually on subscription. If an ezine asks you to subscribe, simply providing an email address will automatically sign you up and the ezine will be delivered via email for you to read at your leisure. An ezine can be an online version of a print periodical or it could be a regularly published electronic magazine, newsletter, journal or report that exists solely online.

Some of the markets listed in this handbook have an online presence as well as a print version, which means they have a website where they will reproduce a certain amount of published material or database back issues of the magazine. Most of these sites do not make extra payments for reproducing material (although there are exceptions) but it does provide much needed exposure to a broader audience. Most of the markets listed in the handbook are produced digitally, either in the form of an ezine, email newsletter, or in downloadable format. Some pay, some don't. However, there are many literary ezines that are a benchmark of quality in the new internet writing industry. By literary, I am referring to quality fiction.

The ezines/magazines included in this handbook have been chosen for a number of reasons:
- General interest
- Writing information
- Markets
- Payment

Obviously, there are many, many ezines that have not been listed. I have had to be selective as there are so many! It is clear that the most highly paid markets are those that have print versions, and the lowest paid markets are often the 'literary' ezines in whatever genre. Within these general categories, there are a number of sub-categories that the markets have been broken into, each are marked by a particular symbol (these symbols appear after the title of the ezine) to distinguish each category:

- Literary - **(L)**
- Non-fiction - **(NF)**
- Genre - **(G)**
- Content providers - **(CP)**

For simplicity's sake the ezines have been listed alphabetically by title, with the URL of the site, and a general description of the ezine's content. Listed underneath the content description are the ezine's statistics where available, these include the category they fall into, frequency of publication, contact details and payment, etc.

Some ezines include all genres, and this is indicated by the symbols. The handbook lists a few titles that provide content for other sites to make use of, which means your material will be posted on the site for sale to another party and in some cases you can set the price. Some sites are good sources of information for writers as well as providing possible markets, but again there can be a large amount of crossover material. Some of the ezines/websites listed have been given a '*' in front of the title, which means they are the ezines which are considered to be particularly good.

The non-fiction sites have been chosen for a number of reasons:

- Their payment rates are particularly high.
- They offer a good idea of what markets are available out there if you are prepared to look for them.
- They have websites where material may be re-published.
- They provide an overview of what is expected of the freelance writer in today's hard nosed business community. Although you may not wish to submit material to them, studying the guidelines and the individual websites of each listing will enable you to compare different approaches and requirements.

The literary/genre ezines have been chosen for the following reasons:

- Literary content.
- They are obvious leaders in the field in terms of vision, overall design, and inspiration for writers.
- General resources.

Payment for material varies greatly on the internet as with print based markets. Many ezines have good scales of payment, others pay flat rates, some per word. It is clear though that there is a good living to be made if you can apply yourself to the task of producing well-written material; this is the key to success.

It must also be noted that without access to the World Wide Web a large proportion of the markets around the world, and many of those listed in this handbook, would be unavailable to the writer.

The print-based magazines have been listed to illustrate the markets available internationally; detailed study of their material is possible because they have websites, which is good news for the writer. It means they no longer have to dig deep to buy copies of magazines to study content, they can simply access the site. In many of these examples it would be impossible for writers to buy copies of the magazine they are hoping to contribute to because they are produced and distributed overseas.

It is not quite so easy to identify readership of ezines on the internet. However, if you study the material on the site carefully you should be able to assess what type of readership the ezine attracts and what sort of material they require. Often specific likes and dislikes will be posted clearly in the writer's guidelines on the site; it is important to read these carefully. You can also gain invaluable insight by reading any editorials posted on the site by individual editors. They quite often list personal preferences, and what they expect from prospective contributors. Also read the 'Mission Statement' if they have one, FAQ's and any information about the people who run the site in the 'About Us' section.

HOW TO ASSESS A WEBSITE

What makes a good website for writers?

The attributes that make a good website can be difficult to assess, but for writers it is probably content, which is why they spend a lot of time searching for good writing sites. 'Content is King' is a common phrase on the internet, but it appears that it is the *quality* of that content that keeps people going back for more. If a site provides trustworthy, fresh content that is updated on a regular basis, then users will know to bookmark the site.

Useful tips for website assessment

You must be able to assess the content on the site you are visiting and there are a number of ways you can do this:

- When you visit a site, check when it was last updated. It was updated three years ago then you know the content has not changed since then.
- If you bookmark a site and go back a few months later and notice that the content is exactly the same as when you last visited, then you know the information on that site has remained unchanged.
- Check that the site has good email links. If you can't find the information you want you need to be able to query someone who can provide you with the details you are looking for, i.e. whether you can submit material or get guidelines.
- Check the links provided on the site. If they are dead links, or links take you to sites that no longer exist or sites that have also not been updated recently, then you will know the original site is not being checked properly.
- If you notice that there are spelling mistakes and grammatical errors on the pages of the site, or incomplete material has been published then you may have cause for concern about the validity of the site's material.

- Is the content easy to read and can you access other pages on the site quickly and easily? Are there plenty of text and graphic links that take you where you want to go and more importantly bring you back again?
- Is it hard to find the information you want?
- Good writing sites are happy to share their basic knowledge for free. There are so many writing sites on the internet that a writer would be hard pushed not to find multiple resources. Most good writing related websites are happy to share this information.

There are some writing sites that provide essential resources for writers that will not change because of the very nature of this information. Advice they may give on how to submit a manuscript to a publisher will not have changed very much, but a list of publishers may have changed a great deal as new ones pop up and others disappear.

What does a good website provide?

Good websites should reflect the interactive, dynamic and ever changing nature of the new medium of the internet. When assessing the value of a particular site look out for sites that are well constructed, organised and edited, and that reflect original and updated content.

- Sites that are interactive are always helpful, because they allow the user to interact with the site. Look out for forums, message boards, ezine subscriptions that offer updated information regularly from the site, chat rooms which enable you to contact other writers.
- Is there too much information on the pages, forcing you to scroll endlessly down a page, or is it broken up into bite size pieces that are quickly read and absorbed?
- Is the site consistent - it may seem unusual but sites that use the same format for pages are much easier on the eye and give a certain confidence to the reader rather than having to look at a mishmash of page design.
- Is the site just a list of links to other sites with not much detail as to what

you will find when you get there? Most good websites point users to lists that someone else has created; a list of publishers or agents can be very helpful but not if that is all the site contains.

- If the site is selling material, e.g. books, do they have a secure payment facility?
- Is there a good site search facility?

BASIC GUIDELINES

Writing non-fiction for ezines

If you are writing non-fiction then you must bear in mind a number of points before you begin:

- Find gaps in the market.
- Develop saleable ideas.
- Conduct thorough market research.
- Avoid clichéd ideas.
- Don't repeat subjects that have already been covered.
- Query individual editors.
- Read guidelines and submission procedures carefully.
- Subscribe to ezines to get a feel for content, style and market, and study the site.

There are also number of basic rules to follow when writing non-fiction:

- Write informally unless you are writing for a highly technical market, using 'you' instead of 'I' if appropriate.
- Sentences and paragraphs should be short.
- Edit your work.
- Be brief. Offer small pieces of information. Internet users tend to scan the pages rather than read in detail.
- Use sub-headings to divide the piece up into separate ideas.
- Use lists and bullets to break up text and precise information.
- Spell check your work.

- Research your subject area effectively.
- Study the market.

Fiction

Writing fiction for the internet is much the same as writing for print based magazines, - you still need to identify a target market and make sure you are submitting your material to the right place. Once again you must produce well-written, well-crafted, interesting and engaging fiction. Ezines want good fiction and sometimes their standards can be even more rigorous than print-based publications. There are sites that publish anything you send them, but most don't. If they do publish material without regard to quality, they usually state this quite clearly. Many of the ezines listed as 'literary' publish fiction and poetry, and it may be helpful to visit the particular website that produces the ezines to get a feel for what sort of fiction or poetry they produce. If you write purely science fiction, horror or fantasy then you will find many sites that cater exclusively for these genres. But it is still important to study the market, as individual ezines may have particular requirements within that genre. Most of the ezines that publish fiction have specific guidelines and submission procedures to follow. It is important to note the required length of stories they are prepared to publish and stick to their limit. If you don't, they will delete your submission. As with non-fiction it is important to follow all guidelines, particularly submission procedures, and these will vary from ezine to ezine. If in doubt you can query the editor. If the ezine you are interested in contributing to has a print based edition then the guidelines may include submitting either on disk or by more traditional means on A4 paper, or both. Some only accept print submissions.

Finding Markets

Finding markets on the internet is easy; knowing what to do with them when you have found them is another matter.

It is always practical to visit the ezine you are intending to target by going to the website it originates from. Familiarize yourself with the content, style and presentation of the website, read the articles already posted to get a feel for the type of material they accept. This applies to both fiction and non-fiction sites. You need to identify the market and this is the quickest way to do it. There is absolutely no point in submitting a romantic short story to a site that is looking for contemporary, cutting edge fiction or an article about fly-fishing to a business based ezine! It is always sensible to query a particular editor about ideas for articles before you send them. This way you will avoid your work being rejected simply because they have already published a similar article in the recent past.

Submitting your work - guidelines and submission procedures

Usually, ezines that are seeking submissions from writers on the internet provide their own list of guidelines and submission procedures. Some ezines have a very casual approach to submissions, simply asking you to submit material by email. A few have online submission forms for you to use, or ask that you submit material via an email link given on the website; most, however, provide quite detailed guidelines and it is important that you follow them. Many have specific formats, and will instruct you how to submit material, especially artwork and photographs. You will notice also that these sites state very clearly that they will reject any submissions that do not abide by their procedures and guidelines. So don't jeopardise your chances before they have had a chance to look at your material. If you are in doubt then send a query email to the ezine asking for more specific guidelines.

Technical terms explained

The technical terms listed below are to be found in most submission guidelines and although they may sound frightening, they are quite easy to follow and understand once you know what they mean and how to implement them.

• *Please submit any artwork or photographs as a JPEG or GIF attachment.* GIF (Graphic Interchange Format) and JPEG (Joint Photographic Experts Group) are Web graphic formats. GIF is limited to 265 colours so it's best for simple images such as line art, clip art, text and so on. JPEG supports complex images that have many millions of colours, and they are smaller than GIFs, so they take less time to download. The JPEG format compresses digitised photographs and other high-quality images so they are easier to manage. JPEG and GIF formats' account for 99% of all Web imagery. If you have a photograph, image or piece of artwork that you want to use in an article and submit to an ezine or a website you will have to convert your image into one of the two formats after you have scanned the image into your computer. You will need a graphics program that is capable of converting these images into different formats. There are three that are commonly used:

Paint Shop Pro - http://www.jasc.com - an all round graphics program. It can convert graphics and manipulate existing images and create new images.

GraphX - http://group42.com - another good graphics program.

Lview Pro - http://lview.com - it can perform some image manipulation, but is best as a graphics converter.

These programs use basically the same steps to convert an image from one format to another.

1. Select the **File, Open** command, and use the Open dialogue box to open the image file you want to convert.

2. Select the **File, Save As** command. The Save As dialogue box will appear.

3. In the **Save as Type** list, choose either JPEG or GIF. (GIF can also be referred to as CompuServe Graphics Interchange Format).

4. Click **Save**. You will then be able to attach the file to an email or put it onto a disk to send with your submission.

• *Copyright: exclusive Worldwide first-time rights for one year, non-exclusive rights after the first year.*

Copyright can be problematic on the internet so you must make sure you are fully aware of what each term refers to. This statement is common, and it simply means that whoever wants to publish your material is given the first rights to do so for one year. This means you cannot publish the material anywhere else for one year after that year you can publish the material elsewhere if you choose. It is a way of keeping the material exclusive to them for a period of time.

- **Submissions can be made in several formats: plain ASCII text is preferred, although we will accept RTF (Microsoft's Rich Text), Microsoft Word (preferably Word 5 for Macintosh), and HTML formats.**

There are several ways of saving text in the word processing facility on your computer that will comply with required formats for submission.

ASCII - is an acronym for American Standard Code for Interface Interchange. It is a file format that contains no text formatting so it is transferable between different operating systems and programmes and is universally used for exchanging information between computers. You can use notepad for text that does not require formatting and is smaller than 64k. Notepad opens and saves text in ASCII format (text-only) format only. For files larger than 64k you can use WordPad.

Microsoft Word provides file format converters for many programs and for several text-only file formats.

RTF - Microsoft's Rich Text File. Rich Text Format (RTF) saves all formatting. Converts formatting to instructions that other programmes can read and interpret.

HTML - (Hypertext Markup Language, primarily used to code text files on the web). Converts documents to and from HTML format. Supports all versions up to HTML 2.0, some Internet Explorer and Netscape Navigator extensions.

Word 5 for Macintosh - Microsoft Word for the Macintosh Versions 4.x and 5.x. (Can be used to save documents in these file formats. No converter is required for opening these formats in Word 97.)

Text only - Saves text without its formatting. Converts all section breaks, page breaks, and new line characters to paragraph marks. Uses the ANSI character set. Select this format only if the destination program cannot read any of the other available file formats.

- **Submissions are preferred via email with the work within the body of the email message. However, attachments, such as Word 6.0 (. Doc) or text (. txt) are accepted as well.**

This means they will accept files attached to an email or alternatively the material pasted into the body of an email. To paste material into the body of an email, simply open your original document, copy the entire text and paste it into the message box (body) of your email. To attach a file to an email, simply start a new message, click the attach button and open the folder where your file is saved, open the file and click on the selected material. This will automatically put the file as an attachment to your email. You can then go on to write your email, put the address in the address box and send.

• **If necessary, italics may be indicated by use of the following characters: [I]...[/I].**
<I> and </I> are HTML codes that immediately convert the text into italics. If you are sending material as text only, any formatting will be lost, this means that any italics or bold or any other changes to text will not appear in the document. If you want to indicate that certain words should be in italics or bold then you must use the appropriate HTML tags to indicate this. If you want to indicate that certain text should be in bold then use the tags: <B> </B>. Insert the text in between the tags.

• **Please put the words "EDITORIAL SUBMISSIONS" in the subject line of the email.**
Simply insert the words "Editorial Submissions" in the subject line of the email. This is so that whoever you are submitting work to will instantly recognise that your email is a submission rather than anything else.

• **Also acceptable is a 3.5-inch IBM-compatible disk, double or high density, with files in Microsoft Word (preferred) or WordPerfect. If you work in any other word-processing software, please convert your files to Word, WordPerfect, or text (ASCII).**
They simply want the text on a floppy disk, but you must make sure that the disk is double or high density, and IBM compatible. Floppy disks come in all shapes and sizes and it is just a question of buying the right ones.

• **File size should be no more than 500k.**
This means they will not accept any files over a certain size, in this case 500k. You can check on the size of the file you are sending in My Documents. Simply click on **File** and then **Open**. Once your folders are displayed open the folder that contains your file. Click on the icon along the top of the box that says **Details** and all the file sizes will appear.

- ***Resolution should be no higher than 150 dpi with an optimum***

Dpi stands for 'dots per inch', a unit used to measure the resolution of a printer. The more dots per inch the sharper an image appears. This also applies to the quality of an image in JPEG or GIF format. When saving your photograph or picture in JPEG or GIF format you can set the resolution to the required depth.

- ***No simultaneous or multiple submissions***

Don't submit the material to another ezine/magazine at the same time, or submit more than one piece of work at a time.

Submissions

These sites list general guidelines and submission procedures for a vast range of markets.

Writer's Digest
www.writersdigest.com
Good source of general information. Market of the day, The Insider's Guide to the Writing Life and the Hot List.

WritingNow.com
www.writingnow.com
Devoted to helping writers market their work.

4journalism.com
www.4journalism.com
Provides many resources for journalists and would-be journo's. Job listing and more.

4literature.com
www.4literature.com
Helpful sites for writers in general. List many other guides all in the same format, i.e. 4authors.com, 4fiction.com, etc.

Guidelines

Many of the sites listed below are databases of guidelines, which makes it easier to track down specific editorial demands. These sites often provide lists of publications and markets.

Writers Writer

www.writerswrite.com/guidelines
Writer's Guidelines Directory. Searchable database of guidelines by publication name, keywords, markets and manuscript type.

Writer's Guidelines Links

www.inkspot.com
List of markets by magazine and ezine listed alphabetically.

Writer's Market

www.writersmarket.com/index-paymarkets99.html
Subscribe to the newsletter, which lists freelance jobs, listings and paying markets, delivered to your email box every Wednesday.

The Write Market

www.writemarket.com
Published by Christopher Reynaga. Resource markets for writers.

On-writing.com

www.on-writing.com/resource.html
Using the web to its fullest potential. Ezines, resources and links.

The Writers Place

www.awoc.com
Writing for dollars. Issues twice a month - free.

The markets
[An a-z listing]

Afterimage (NF)
http://www.vsw.org/afterimage

Afterimage is a non-profit bi-monthly journal of photography, independent film, video and alternative publishing, which includes visual books, electronic imaging and the internet. Each issue contains a wide range of critical features, reviews, and essays, as well as up-to-date news coverage of issues and events that affect the media arts community. They also publish reports on festivals, conferences and other events, review exhibitions, films and books and publish scholarly features. They are looking for work that reflects multiple perspectives rather than a one-dimensional approach to a subject. You are strongly advised to avoid jargon or self-promotion. 80% freelance. Welcomes new writers.

Category: Non fiction - visual arts/alternative publishing.
Frequency: Bi-monthly.
Contact: afterimg@servtech.com.
Editor: Karen vanMeenen.
Cost: Subscription $30.
Payment: Afterimage pays five cents a word for articles, with a maximum of $100 for news, reports and reviews; $150 for essays; and $300 for features. Payment is made after publication, not acceptance; cheques may take some months to process.

Feature writers receive 10 free copies of the issue; review, report; essay and news writers receive five. Writers also receive a half-price subscription voucher.
Language: English.
Rights: Joint copyright for all print and electronic use of entire issues as well as single articles.
Reply Time: ASAP and publishes articles 8-16 weeks after acceptance.

Guidelines and submission procedures:

Afterimage accepts both commissions and unsolicited manuscripts. With unsolicited manuscripts include writing samples and an SAE if you would like the manuscript returned. All writers are encouraged to discuss article ideas with the editors before submitting finished articles. They do not reprint previously published pieces.

Articles: Must be formatted in Microsoft Word, version 5.0, and submitted on a standard 3 1/2-inch disk for Macintosh. Always mail a double-spaced hard copy as well.

Features: Ranging from 4,000-10,000 words, feature articles may be original investigative reporting or scholarly research; they may be biographies of or interviews with important media artists or critics; they may use an event, exhibition, book or video, etc. as a jumping-off point for a discussion of larger economic, political and cultural issues. Use of endnotes is expected but not strictly required.

Reviews: Reviews are generally 700-1500 words. They may cover individual or group exhibitions, installations, screenings and performances; or they may examine one or more media arts publications. References should be placed within the text, though endnotes are permitted.

Essays: Like the feature in terms of prominence and scope, but more like the review in terms of timeliness and length (they range from 1500-3000 words), an essay may be written in a more "subjective" voice and it may be on or about virtually any subject in the domain of media arts and cultural criticism. Most essays are written on commission, though Afterimage will consider unsolicited manuscripts. Endnotes are explicitly discouraged.

Reports: This section includes articles (700-1500 words) about particular conferences, symposia, film and video festivals and other formal gatherings. A good report will provide both an account and an analysis of the event. Endnotes are discouraged.

News: Afterimage publishes news stories on funding, legislation, activism and institutional restructuring, as well as obituaries and other topics of importance to our readership. Although most news items are written by Afterimage staff, longer news articles (1500-4000 words) are actively solicited from outside writers. References should by placed within the text, though endnotes are permitted in longer news articles.

Anotherealm (G)

http://Anotherealm.com/

Anotherealm publishes speculative fiction including science fiction, fantasy and horror. They do publish flash fiction (short fiction) up to 200 words. If your story is rejected they have a number of services to provide you with feedback. These cost $2 and $4 respectively.

Category: Science Fiction.
Frequency: Weekly.
Contact: goldstrm@tu.infi.net
Editor: Jean Goldstrom.
Publisher: Jean Goldstrom.
Cost: Free.
Language: English.
ISSN: 1524-7120.
Rights: Query editor.
Payment: US$10 per story, upon acceptance.
Reply Time: ASAP.

Guidelines and submission procedures:

Anotherealm will have one open submission period per year. The next period will start Jan. 1, 2001 and continue through March 31, 2001. They accept submissions only during those three months.

Send them a story - speculative fiction, no more than 5,000 words. And by speculative fiction they mean science fiction, fantasy, magic realism, or anything that isn't slice-of-life or journalistic. No simultaneous submissions.

How to send: Their favourite format is ASCII, in an email letter to the editor. (editor@anotherealm.com). Second favourite is snail mail, typed, double-spaced, your name and the story name on each page. Include a stamped return envelope if you want your submission returned. If you don't want it returned, tell them.
Send your Mss. to: Jean Goldstrom, 287 Gano Ave, Orange Park FL 32073.

Flash Fiction: Anotherealm is now accepting flash fiction (200 words maximum) for display in Beyond Anotherealm. Unfortunately, there is no payment. Send submissions to flashfiction@anotherealm.com and they may post it for a month.

Back Brain Recluse (G)

http://www.bbr-online.com/magazine

Back Brain Recluse magazine publishes some of the most startling and daring SF currently being written, and has developed a cult following around the world through their policy of emphasising the experimental and un-commercial end of the form. Recent contributors have included Richard Kadrey, Paul Di Filippo, Michael Moorcock, Misha, Don Webb and Mark Rich, as well as many exciting new names making their first professional appearance. Welcomes new writers. Website 100% freelance.

Category: Science Fiction.
Frequency: Published irregularly.
Contact: Email magazine@bbr-online.com (inquiries only).
Editor: Chris Reed.
Publisher: BBR.
Cost: Subscription.
Language: English.
Rights: First English Language rights. No reprints.
Payment: Pays £10 ($15) per 1,000 words. Pays around $30 US for art/photos on publication per black and white full page used. Pays on publication.
Reply Time: Replies within two months or longer.

Guidelines and submission procedures:

Guidelines by mail with SASE/IRC, by email, and online. Familiarity with the magazine is strongly advised. Email submissions will not be considered. Submit two International Reply Coupons (IRCs) plus disposable copy for non-UK submissions.

Photos/Art: Illustrations of stories are commissioned and artists are invited to send samples of their work for consideration.

BackPacker magazine (NF)
http://www.backpacker.com

BackPacker is concerned with articles and information about wilderness travel, primarily foot-based and in North America. They are looking for high quality photographs and inspiring stories. They are interested in low impact uses of wilderness. Another peculiar choice but they pay well. This is a sample of a market that although specific to North America is just one of many magazines in its genre that could provide a good market for your work, particularly if you are into hiking.

Category: Non-fiction print magazine.
Frequency: 9 issues annually, one of which is the Gear Guide (March).
Circulation: 265,000.
Editor: Tom Shealey.
Language: English.
Payment: They pay $0.60 to $1.00 per word, depending upon the complexity and demands of the article, as well as the proven experience of the writer. Their pay rates for photography varies on how the photograph is used, and at what size: Cover photos: $550-800. Photo use inside magazine: $100-400 (depends upon size and placement). Assignment day rate: $400-450.
Rights: In general they pay on acceptance and buy all rights.
Reply Time: Allow 6-8 weeks for replies.

Guidelines and submission procedures:

As always, you should carefully study several issues of the magazine before submitting a query. The best articles have style, depth, emotional impact, and take-away value for the reader.

While staff and regular contributors write a large portion of Backpacker, they encourage freelance authors to submit query letters for features and departments. Freelancers write approximately 20% of their features and over half of their departments. Direct your efforts toward establishing a working relationship with them via department assignments first.

Destinations: Backpacker uses pieces that go beyond a mere description of a trail or place. Typical word count is 1250-1750 words, plus a full Expedition sidebar (contact, permit, season, hazards, map, guidebook, and other useful information.)

Personality: Plenty of unique personalities exist to write about. Colorful, controversial, historically significant, amusing, unusual, or unique people are what they're looking for, especially those that have a direct impact on how or where others hike.

Technique: Skill-based articles in Backpacker feature high levels of take-away value. A good technique piece also has information relevant to all skill levels (e.g. beginner, intermediate, and advanced hikers).

Gear: Field-Tests and comparative gear reviews are always written by writers they have worked with before. If you're interested in writing such articles, start by querying one of the gear editors about the Outfitting department. See 'Departments' below:

Departments: Freelancers most often break into Backpacker's pages in the departments. These shorter assignments (100 to 1200 words) have specific topics and focus: see website.

Queries: With the exception of Backcountry, they prefer queries to completed works. Send samples of your published work with your first query. Include an SAE if your samples must be returned.

All queries should be sent to the appropriate editor at the following address: Backpacker, 33 E. Minor Street, Emmaus, PA 18098.

Banking Strategies Magazine (NF)
http://www.bai.org/bankingstrategies

Magazine covering financial services from a strategic and managerial perspective. This is a rather esoteric field, so you have to have a certain amount of expertise to give their stories the sophisticated polish they require. They need writers who can think thematically and shape their stories within an analytical framework. Their standards are high and only a few writers end up working for them on a regular basis. Best way to get insight into the publication is look at the website and study some of the freelance copy. 50% freelance. Works with new writers if they have a strong financial services background.

Category: Non fiction.
Frequency: Bi-monthly.
Contact: kcline@bai.org.
Editor: Kenneth Cline.
Publisher: BAI.
Cost: Free online subscription.
Language: English.
ISSN: 1091-7357.
Rights: Buys all rights. No reprints.
Payment: Pays $1.20/word for features to 2,500 words. Payment on acceptance (after editing and based on post-editing word count). Publishes ms 1 month after acceptance.
Reply Time: ASAP.

Guidelines and submission procedures:

Detailed guidelines by email. Needs writers with good news reporting skills combined with analytical, magazine-style writing.

Submit bio and clips by mail or email. If pitching a story idea, send synopsis only. **Photos/Art:** They ask writers to help find charts and tables to illustrate stories.

Circle of Poets (G)

http://www.taddgroup.com/poetry_newsletter.htm

Free poetry newsletter where poets share their works with each other and the world. Also features Calls For Poetry - a place to find a market for your poetry or enter a competition. Past issues are archived on the site.

Category: Poetry.
Frequency: Daily.
Contact: taddgroup@aol.com
Editor: E. H. Morrison.
Publisher: TADD Publishing Group.
Cost: Free.
Language: English.
Payment: Any content used in their publications from outside sources is always given proper credit in the form of a by-line, tag line and/or link.
Rights: All contributors retain full copyright to their work.
Reply Time: 48 hours

Guidelines and submission procedures:

This is a forum to share your poetry with other subscribers and the world. Each day a new poet is featured, along with one of their poems. There are no restrictions as far as content or form.

The Circle of Poets Newsletter is meant to promote not only the art of poetry but also, the poets themselves.

Computer Currents (NF)
http://www.currents.net

Computer Currents is a source of help and information for PC and Mac business users of all types, focusing on real world solutions to business users, showing them how to buy products, what products to buy, where to buy them, and how to use them. Their readers run small businesses, manage mid-sized firms and serve as department heads in large corporations. Although their style is informal and lively, every story has to deliver practical help, opinions and resources to the reader. Most of their readers use PCs and Windows 95. About 20 percent of their readers use the Mac.

Category: Non-fiction.
Frequency: Bi-weekly.
Circulation: 612,000 readers; "pass along" readership is nearly 1.5 million.
Editor: Robert Luhn, Editor-in-Chief.
Contact: Free rluhn@compcurr.com.
Cost: Free.
Language: English.
Payment: Payment: $1,500 to $2,000. All payment is upon publication.
Rights: Buys all rights.
Reply Time: ASAP.

Guidelines and submission procedures:

Freelance opportunities: Computer Currents' editorial falls into three categories: product news ("Currents"), cover stories and features, and various review/how-to/opinion columns.

Do not submit stories for their columns—these are written by specific contributing editors.

Freelance opportunities come down to two areas: short reviews for their Previews & Reviews section and feature length cover stories and secondary features. Previews & Reviews runs short pieces (300 to 600 words) on shipping and pre-release (beta) software and hardware. Previews and reviews should be lively, critical, and to the point.

Cover stories range from 2,500 to 3,500 words and fall into one of several categories:

How-to: Shows readers how to solve a specific problem.

Technology introduction/overview: Explains a new technology to readers and gives them a clear idea of the benefits, pitfalls, and costs.

Consumer investigation: Explores issues affecting how consumers buy, use, or have products repaired.

Buyer's guides: Shows readers how to buy products or services and how to protect themselves. A detailed table listing products or services usually accompanies a buyer's guide and key specs/features readers should be on the lookout for.

Reviews: These pieces are either round-ups of products in a certain category (great shareware, best games) or focused looks at a specific genre (such as Netscape plug-ins). Reviews don't include speed tests typically, but do involve assessing the product's design, operation, ease of use/set-up, and the company's service and support.

Contact: Robert Luhn, Editor-in-Chief, rluhn@compcurr.com or Melissa Riofrio, Senior Editor, mriofrio@compcurr.com Rights we buy: First North American rights, right to post piece on their website (www.currents.net), non-exclusive reprint rights. Also run shorter (1,000 word) secondary features on all of the above topics. These features pay $700+. We buy the same rights as cover stories.

How to submit: Query before submitting any feature or review. Query with photocopied clips of your work that has appeared in other publications. A self-addressed, stamped envelope with sufficient postage should accompany all queries/submissions. Otherwise you will not receive a reply. Queries and clips can be sent to: Computer Currents, 1250 Ninth St. Berkeley, CA 94710. Email queries are acceptable.

Comrades (L)
http://www.safesurfer.co.uk/ezine/index2.htm

Provides exposure for new and established writers by offering them a place where their work will be seen and read. UK based. Friendly site, with a good welcoming message that should put contributors at ease. Archived copies of the ezine are readily available. Publishes good quality fiction and poetry.

Category: Literary
Frequency: Updated regularly.
Contact: verian@safesurfer.co.uk
Editor: Verian Thomas.
Cost: Free.
Language: English.
Rights: Query editor.
Payment: Non paying, non-profit ezine.
Reply Time: ASAP.

Guidelines and submission procedures:

The following information must be included in your email - your name, email address and URL of your own site (if applicable). Do not just send them the URL of your own site. Submissions accepted only in the body of the email (no attachments accepted to avoid compatibility and software problems). Just copy and paste it into your email (Note: other than JPEG attachments)

Short stories: Maximum length of 5000 words. If you have something longer that you would like to submit, email a query in the first instance.
Poetry: Only submit an example of poetry, up to 5 poems.
Artwork: Please submit any artwork with a maximum file size of 100k. (This can be larger if it is published and may be sent as a. JPEG attachment.)
Non-fiction & Memoirs: Are gladly accepted. They also publish and welcome guest Journal entries.

Submissions should be sent to the relevant editor listed below:

Short Stories Editor - Deborah Swain

Poetry Editor - Claudine Moreau

Non-fiction/ Memoirs Editor - Verian Thomas

Italia Pages Editor - Valentina Mazzei

Art Editor - Daniel Mcanulty

B & W Editor - If you wish to have your own B & W website within the Comrades Writing Community then please email an introductory note, telling them something about yourself and your work along with a couple of examples, how many pieces of work you wish to include on the website.

*CyberAge Adventures (G)
http://www.cyberageadventures.com/

Cyber Age Adventures is constantly seeking groundbreaking, thought-provoking fiction that reinvents the superhero. One of the best genre sites on the web, although it does take a long time to load, but be patient, it's worth it. Recently voted the third best fiction magazine on the internet by an online poll.

Category: Redefining the comic book hero.
Frequency: Updated Regularly.
Contact: Editor@cyberageadventures.com
Tom Waltz, Submissions Editor: tom@cyberageadventures.com
Editor: Frank Fradella.
Cost: Buy discounted copies from the site.
Language: English.
ISSN: #1524-9883.
Rights: They buy one-time publication and print rights.
Payment: They offer you a choice of compensation methods. They pay $0.02 to $0.05 per word depending on your previous writing credits. Alternately, they offer you the chance to be a hero yourself by allowing them to make a donation in your name to the charity of your choice. Please specify which charity you would prefer if you choose this payment method.
Reply Time: Acceptance letters may take up to four weeks. Rejection letters usually within one week.

Guidelines and submission procedures:

An Online Tutorial exists on the website if you'd like to learn how to write for Cyber Age Adventures.

All characters represented in your stories must be original. This is not a magazine of fan fiction.

Format: All entries must be in English and should be submitted in the body of an email. Double space in between paragraphs and do not indent. Submissions may be short-short fiction (up to 1,500 words) or short fiction (no longer than 3,000 words).

They no longer accept serial submissions.

Author information: Include your name, mailing address, email address and word count at the top of every submission. Also include a brief, one-paragraph biography of yourself that they may include on the website. If you have a website you would like them to link your name to, include that information as well.

Themes: Cyber Age Adventures is constantly seeking groundbreaking, thought-provoking fiction that reinvents the superhero. They are looking for stories about people with themes and conflicts with which their readers can identify.

Your story will appear on the website for 90 days and will be mailed to all subscribers. Often, guest artists create illustrations for the stories they buy. The rights to those illustrations, and their likenesses, remain those of the artist. They simply copyright the issue that it appears in.

Submission: Submit all stories to Submissions@cyberageadventures.com with the word "Submission:" followed by your story title as the subject heading.

Artist's Submission Guidelines for Cyber Age Adventures:

Format: All submissions must be done electronically as an attached file to an email in JPEG format. Resolution should be no higher than 150 dpi with an optimum file size of no more than 500k.

Artist Information: Include your name, mailing address, email address and the characters depicted in your drawing at the top of every submission. Also include a brief, one paragraph biography of yourself that they may include on our website. If you have a website you would like them to link your name to, please include that information as well.

Themes: Cyber Age Adventures is constantly seeking ground breaking, thought-provoking fiction that reinvents the superhero. A unique style and individuality is what impresses them the most.

Copyrights: This is a work for hire, allowing them the electronic rights so that they may publish the piece on the website and print rights, so that they may publish the piece in their annual anthology.

Compensation: For the illustration itself, they pay a nominal fee of $20 per accepted illustration. In the case of merchandising (coffee mugs, tee shirts, etc.), you receive 25% (or equal portion thereof in the case of multiple artists) of all profits from the sale of any goods with your work on it. The royalties are paid quarterly.

Response Time: They generally reply to art submissions within a few days at most.

Fiction Writer's Guideline (NF)
http://www.fictionwriters.com

FWC offers a wealth of information to writers as well as providing a good market for their writing. Membership entitles you to a number of benefits, including their newsletter, a free critique service, email courses and a lot more. It is also one of the better known sites for writers on the internet. Includes the hardcopy newsletter, Fiction Writer's Guidelines, and Tidbits, an online newsletter for members.

Category: Information for writers.
Frequency: Updated regularly.
Contact: BCamenson@aol.com.
Editor: Ms. Blythe Camenson.
Cost: Free.
Language: English.
Rights: One-time rights or reprint rights.
Payments: Fees currently range from $1 to $25, depending upon length and subject matter. Payment is within two weeks after publication. As circulation increases, so will writers' fees.
Reply Time: ASAP.

Guidelines and submission procedures:

Topics: How-to Articles offering practical advice on the craft of writing fiction and practical tips and advice on getting published. Success Stories, Interviews with Authors, Agents, and Editors. No personal essays.
Word count: From 250 to 1200 words.
Manuscript submission: All articles will be considered "on spec." Please submit complete manuscript. All manuscripts must be typed and double-spaced, with the exact word count typed in the upper right hand corner of the first page. Be sure to include your name, address, telephone number, and email address. An SAE must accompany all submissions.
Author interviews: You are free to choose the authors you interview. The only

requirements are that he or she is an author of fiction and has been at least moderately successful. Ask each author how he or she became interested in writing as a profession and detail how he or she got started. How did they get their first book published: did they go through an agent, or submit to editors themselves? How many places did they submit their manuscript to until it was accepted? Any interesting anecdotes/feedback/comments in the process? How were they notified of their first sale: phone/mail etc? How much did they get paid: advance/royalty % for their first sale? For the latest sale? Advice to aspiring writers. Next project in the works?

Agent interviews: Agents interviewed must handle fiction, be open to new writers, have room to add new clients to their list, and must not charge a reading fee. The following information must be obtained during your interview: genres they are most interested in; how they prefer to be approached, i.e. telephone, query; what they want to see, i.e. synopses, the first 3 chapters/50 pages, etc.; response time; recent sales (if available); commission charged; any photocopying/fax fees, etc.; advice to FWC members.

Editor interviews: Editors interviewed must handle fiction and be willing to accept un-agented submissions. The following information must be obtained during your interview: genres they are interested in; how they want to be approached initially, response time, submission do's and don'ts, advances, royalties, advice, etc.

History Today (NF)
http://admin@historytoday.com

History Today is an independent monthly published in the UK. So if you have a passion for history then you will find a good market for your work here. They offer a good variety of articles on a vast range of historical subjects. The website includes samples of articles taken from the magazine so you can get a good idea of what sort of material they are looking for fairly easily.

Category: Non-fiction.
Frequency: Monthly.
Contact: p.furtado@historytoday.com.
Editor: Peter Furtado.
Cost: £3.25.
Language: English.
Rights: Query editor.
Payment: Payment by arrangement.
Reply Time: ASAP.

Guidelines and submission procedures:

History Today does accept unsolicited articles to be considered for publication, although the large majority of articles published in the magazine are commissioned. However, due to the number of unsolicited articles they receive, they ask that if you are interested in submitting an article to them send a 200-300 word synopsis of the article in question.

Ideas for articles can be emailed to them online from the website, or sent to: editorial@historytoday.com.

Hope magazine (NF)

http://www.hopemag.com

Hope magazine has a distinct style. They are primarily interested in making the world a better place and looking for writers who can contribute to this process by becoming part of the solution themselves. It may seem a rather overblown sentiment but most of their articles are extremely thought provoking. They deal with subjects including health, ageing, work and even the meaning of life, with a perspective that is quite uplifting. Study of the website is strongly recommended.

Category: Non-fiction.
Frequency: Updated regularly.
Editor: Jon Wilson.
Contact: kimr@hopemag.com.
Publisher: Jon Wilson, Editor & Publisher, jon@hopemag.com.
Language: English.
Payment: Fifty cents per word for text, and about $300 for a full-page editorial Photograph.
Rights: They purchase serial rights for one-time use of text and images, except in cases of prior agreement by the parties.
Reply Time: ASAP.

Guidelines and submission procedures:

Features run from 1,500 to 6,000 words, depending on subject, and they are always willing to integrate sidebar material where it adds substance. Essays on varied subjects run from 1,000 to 4,000 words in length. Departments include Signs of Hope: notes and dispatches, generally ranging from 200 to 600 words, in which good and great works and ideas are reported.

Aspirations: 1,000 to 1,500-word reports on individuals or groups in their teens (or younger (who are engaged in works worthy of our recognition).

Arts of Hope: 1,000 to 2,000-word reviews and discussions of music, art, and literature related to hope.

Book Reviews: 500 to 800-word pieces devoted primarily to non-fiction works in widely diverse subject areas related to struggle and triumph.

Last Hope: 1,000 to 2,000-word essays on ways in which individuals have given special meaning to their last moments on Earth (for themselves or others).

Photography and Illustration: Hope is a strongly visual magazine. Their editorial photography and illustration is primarily black & white, although they do use some colour. They are very interested in, and committed to the photo essay form, and enthusiastically encourage photographers and photojournalists to query them with ideas.

They also run two images in each issue, one on the first page, and one on the last, called Prologue and Parting Shot.

They welcome queries via fax, email: info@hopemag.com, and U.S. Mail. Representative writing samples should accompany your queries if they are unfamiliar with your work. Manuscripts should be typed, double-spaced, and accompanied by diskettes whenever possible. They use Microsoft Word for Windows 6.0, although they are usually able to open and work with other PC and Mac files. Unsolicited manuscripts will not be returned unless accompanied by a self-addressed, stamped envelope. Hope magazine Kimberly Ridley, Senior Editor (features) Frances Lefkowitz, Assistant Editor (departments) P.O. Box 160, Naskeag Road, Brooklin, ME 04616

I Love Cats Magazine (NF)

http://www.iluvcats.com

If you love cats then obviously this is the one for you! The magazine is 80% free-lance so there is a good chance of finding a niche for your work and they welcome new writers and ideas.

Category: Non-fiction.
Frequency: Bi-monthly.
Contact: yankee@dancom.com.
Editor: Lisa M. Allmendinger.
Publisher: Grass Roots Publishing.
Cost: Sample $4.50. Subscription $26; $36 Canada.
Language: English.
Rights: Buys all rights. No reprints.
Payment: Pays $50-200 depending on the story for 500-1,500 words. Pays on publication. Artwork: Pays $25-250 for a cover. Short fillers: $25. Non-fiction: $50.
Reply Time: Responds in 1-2 months.

Guidelines and submission procedures:

Guidelines by mail with SAE, at website, or by email. Any stories that deal with cats. Fiction and non-fiction are published. No poetry. No tributes to dead cats. Submit complete ms or query with SAE.

Send a paragraph or two about your idea or the finished piece. Send printed copy, but also a 3-1/2 inch disc in a format compatible with Windows 95. No outlines.

Stories - preferably with photos or drawings - of 1,000 words, ideally 500-700 words.

Colour slides and colour photos are also welcome.

Inkspot (L)
www.inkspot.com

Includes 'Inklings' a free Bi-weekly newsletter including market information, articles, and how-to tips for writers. Good all round website and extremely useful newsletter, good page of staff contacts for easy access to individual editors. This is one of the best sites for writers on the internet. They advertise widely and have established a definite niche in the writing market.

Category: Literary newsletter.
Frequency: Dependent upon publication.
Contact: info@inkspot.com.
Editor: Debbie Ridpath Ohi.
Cost: Free.
Language: English.
Rights: For Inklings (newsletter), they ask for exclusive world wide first-time rights plus non-exclusive archival rights (e.g. they keep back issues of Inklings online).

For Inkspot (website), they ask for exclusive world-wide first-time rights for one year, non-exclusive rights after the first year.

Payment: Payment is 6c/wd, U.S. funds, on publication. If they choose to publish the article in both Inkspot and Inklings, pay is an additional 3c/wd. Please note that receiving a go-ahead on a query does not necessarily mean they will publish the article.
Reply Time: Up to two weeks for a query, four weeks for a submission.

Guidelines and submission procedures:

You can get a copy of the current guidelines by sending an email to guidelines@inkspot.com. The most important guideline for writers wishing to write for Inkspot and its related publications is to familiarise yourself with material they have already purchased. There are four areas/publications, which currently accept material; some have separate guidelines.

Global Writers Ink: Biweekly international marketing newsletter for writers. Editor: Moira Allen. For guidelines, send a blank email to guidelinesglobal@inkspot.com

The Ink Blotter a.k.a. "The Writer's Sanity Break": Short fiction and poetry for writers. Editor: Christopher Donner. For guidelines, send a blank email to guidelinesblotter@inkspot.com

Inklings: Biweekly newsletter for writers. Editor: Debbie Ridpath Ohi. Associate Editor: Moira Allen. Guidelines below. For back issues, go to http://www.inkspot.com/inklings/

Inkspot: The above three publications are part of Inkspot, a website for writers. They also buy articles and interviews specifically for posting on the website. Editor: Debbie Ridpath Ohi. Associate Editor: Moira Allen. See guidelines below. For past articles go to http://www.inkspot.com/feature/

Always query first. Include a brief outline, your writing credits (if any), your website URL (if you have one), estimated number of words, and a brief sample of your writing style. Query by email only. Send your query within the body of your email message; do not use attachments. Send to submissions@inkspot.com. If you've worked with Inkspot before, tell them.

Format and style:
Use plain ASCII text, no "curly" quotes. Don't indent paragraphs. Instead, separate paragraphs with a blank line.

Length: Average 500-800 wds. Longer pieces may be accepted on rare occasions, but shorter pieces have a better chance of being bought. No two-part articles.

[For a list of available autoresponders and general info about Inkspot, please write to info@inkspot.com]

Inscriptions Magazine (NF)

http://www.inscriptionsmagazine.com

If you haven't heard of Inscriptions then you need to get out more. If you have, then you will know they are one of the biggest ezines for professional writers on the internet. They are particularly interested in articles geared toward writers and editors who freelance and/or telecommute. Each issue features how-to articles, interviews with writers/editors/publishers, job opportunities, paying markets, contests and much more. It is a must for every writer.

Category: Literary.
Frequency: Weekly.
Contact: Editor@inscriptionsmagazine.com
Editor: Jade Walker.
Subscribers: 4,000 plus. Unique users to website per month: 25,800. Hits on average: 153,600.
Cost: Free.
Language: English.
Rights: Inscriptions asks for one time electronic rights to publish the article on the website and in the text-only email version of the magazine. Inscriptions copyrights the issue where the article appears. All other copyrights remain with the author. Upon publication, the author is free to resell or publish the article elsewhere. They do archive articles for one year on the website, but all articles are removable or excluded at the writer's request.
Payment: Articles and Interviews: $40.00, or they will include a 50-word text ad (run within the ezine) or a banner ad (up to 7k) run on the website for up to four weeks.

Humour: $5 for each accepted and published humour items. Payments are made on the first of the month for all articles used in the past 30 days or they will include a 50-word text ad (run within the ezine) or a banner ad (up to 7k) run on the website for one week. Reviews: $5 for each accepted review.
Reply Time: Up to two weeks for a query, four weeks for a submission.

Guidelines and submission procedures:

Articles and Interviews:

Articles must focus on writing or publishing-related issues (including interviews, how to's, troubleshooting, etc.). Articles must be between 500 and 1,500 words. Interviews should be conducted with working writers, authors, writing teachers, editors, agents or publishers. If articles link to websites, they must be formatted with the name of the site, then the URL in parentheses. Ex. Inscriptions

(http://www.inscriptionsmagazine.com). Websites mentioned in articles must be relevant to the topic and available for the public to view. Inscriptions accepts reprints of writing-related articles. Email Jade Walker, Editor of Inscriptions, at Editor@inscriptionsmagazine.com. Use the subject heading "Article Query." Paste the query directly into the message area. Single-space all lines. Put two spaces between paragraphs. Do not indent paragraphs.

Humour: Humour articles must focus on the writing or publishing life. Keep submissions under 1,000 words. Email to Jade Walker, Editor of Inscriptions, at Editor@inscriptionsmagazine.com. Use the subject heading "Humour." Paste it directly into the message area. Single-space all lines. Put two spaces between paragraphs. Do not indent paragraphs. Include your full name, pen name (if preferred), mailing address, phone number and email address.

Book Reviews:

Inscriptions publish five book reviews each week. Reviewers must be published writers, authors or editors. They must be willing to review both print and electronic books with a four-week deadline. Each review is 300-500 words and must be honest and critical. All reviews are assigned; they do not accept reviews from non-staff members. In exchange for reviews, staff writers get to keep the book, and receive $5for each accepted review. Inscriptions archives all book reviews for one year on the website.

Insomnia zine (L)

www.insomniazine.co.uk

Strong London focus. Welcomes reviews, photography, comment, editorial, interviews, artwork, profiles and ideas for future articles. They are interested in anything from an urban/ pop culture angle: contemporary fiction & non-fiction, fashion, clubbing, technology, lifestyle, comedy, travel, fringe culture, the web, London art shows, bars, print zines. Well-designed website with strong interactive features such as chat, message board, newsletter and competitions. Provides a good insight into what makes the capital tick in terms of arts and media, including a directory of events.

Category: Popular culture - ezine.
Frequency: Updated regularly.
Contact: submissions@insomniazine.co.uk.
Editor: Editor: Jo Asker - jo@insomniazine.co.uk.
Cost: Free.
Language: English.
Payment: At present no payment for contributions.
Rights: Writers retains all rights to work.
Reply Time: ASAP.

Guidelines and submission procedures:

All submissions should be sent as email attachments (*. JPEG or *.GIF format for images) to: submissions@insomniazine.co.uk. If selected they will email you a copy of your work with any editorial changes, questions or comments before publication. **What you get:** your own @insomniazine.co.uk email address which you can include in articles to encourage feedback. All this mail will be forwarded directly to your regular email account.

Keep your writing concise. As a web publication they encourage contributors to include relevant links to other sites, newsgroups & mailing lists in their submissions. No poetry. Look over the site to get a feel of what's expected. Email: submissions@insomniazine.co.uk for further details. Phone: 0973 782 802 (international): +44 973 782802. Fax: (national) 0870 0561390 (international) +44 870 0561390.

Other email contacts:
General enquiries: info@insomniazine.co.uk.
Feedback: feedback@insomniazine.co.uk.
Advertising: advertising@insomniazine.co.uk.
Contributions: submissions@insomniazine.co.uk.
Listings: listings@insomniazine.co.uk.
Editor: jo@insomniazine.co.uk.

Interchange (G)

www.aber.ac.uk/~engwww/INTERCHANGE.htm

Interchange, was founded by Richard Marggraf Turley, Tom Hengen and Stuart Kime in 1997. Its aim is to create a hybridization of poetry – published and unpublished poets; famous and anonymous writers – in the form of a journal with no fixed political agenda. Read their mission statement to get an overview of their aims and aspirations.

Category: Poetry.
Frequency: Published twice a year.
Contact: rcm@aber.ac.uk
Editor: Richard Marggraf Turley, Tom Hengen and Stuart Kime.
Publisher: University of Wales, Aberystwyth.
Circulation: 300.
Cost: The most recent edition cost £3.00.
Language: English.
Payment: None.
Rights: Remain with author.
Reply Time: 2 months.

Guidelines and submission procedures:

The editors and advisory board welcomes contributions. Submit three copies of work with a copy on disk, if possible (preferably Word for Windows 6.0 or 2.0). Poems may also be sent as email messages or as email attachments to rcm@aber.ac.uk

Notes and critical essays should not exceed 1500 words and should be prepared to the MHRA stylesheet. Please submit three copies as described above.

The only criteria for work accepted for publication is that it merits praise simply for being a "good poem". This is a very vague term, and one that is defined by the current tastes of the Editorial Board. However, the basic principle stands that no poem will be overlooked.

Subscription and all other enquiries should be directed to:

EZINES

The Editors, Interchange, Department of English, University of Wales, Aberystwyth Hugh Owen Building, Penglais, Aberystwyth, Ceredigion, SY23 3DY, UK.

Intertext (L)
www.intertext.com

InterText is a free, online Bi-monthly fiction magazine. It publishes material ranging from mainstream stories to fantasy to horror to science fiction to humor. InterText has been publishing continuously on the Net since March of 1991. Very professional, no-frills website. Past issues are easily accessible. A selection of the best stories published on the site over the past nine years are available under the heading 'Best Stories'.

InterText publishes in Setext (ASCII text which can also be read as styled text with a Setext browser), PostScript (laser printers), PDF (for Adobe's Acrobat portable document viewer), Newton Book, PalmPilot, and HTML/World Wide Web formats.

Category: Literary ezine.
Frequency: Bi-monthly (issues are released on the 15th of every odd-numbered month.)
Contact: editors@intertext.com.
Editor: Jason Snell and Geoff Duncan.
Cost: Free.
Language: English.
Payment: InterText cannot pay its contributors.
Rights: All writers retain the copyright to their stories. The editor, Jason Snell copyrights each issue, but all future rights to stories remain with the authors.
Reply Time: They mail out acceptances about two weeks before an issue is released and rejection notices either a couple of weeks before an issue is released or just after an issue is released. But response times can be up to eight weeks depending on timing of submissions.

Guidelines and submission procedures:

All genres of writing are considered for publication, as are stories that cross between traditional genre boundaries. InterText has published "mainstream"-style stories, as well as fantasy, humour, science fiction, horror, and everything in-between, including stories that cut across several genres. InterText only accepts original work and cannot publish works using copyrighted characters or settings (e.g. Star Trek).

Stories should be under 15,000 words, though rare exceptions to this rule can be made. They are very selective about longer, serialised works.

Submissions can be made in several formats: plain ASCII text is preferred, although we will accept RTF (Microsoft's Rich Text/Interchange Format, preferably UUEncoded or binhexed), Microsoft Word (preferably Word 5 for Macintosh), and HTML formats. They ask that you try not to submit in any format other than ASCII text, RTF, Microsoft Word, or HTML.

InterText prefers submissions be received via electronic mail. Please include your full name and a stable electronic mail address with all submissions. If you do not have stable email access, please include a mailing address and telephone number.

Send submissions to submissions@intertext.com. Back issues of InterText are available on the website.

Authors are always notified when a story is accepted. They will request biographical information and it is up to you to look for your story in the upcoming issue. At least two InterText editors will edit a story before it appears in the magazine. These edits can be perfunctory, or they can be deep, depending on the story.

Non-fiction and Poetry:

InterText will consider humour, essays, and other non-fiction articles. However, they are primarily a fiction magazine and are very selective with non-fiction pieces. Writers are encouraged to contact the magazine before submitting such material.

They encourage queries about possible stories for their non-fiction 'Need to Know' feature, a brief piece at the back of the magazine that covers a topic in the online world that they think will interest readers. InterText does not accept poetry submissions.

Jackhammer Ezine (G)

http://www.eggplant-productions.com/jackhammer/

Explore life, the universe and everything each week through articles, science fiction, fantasy and horror. The website is a bit bland and difficult to navigate around, and it appears there are no archives on the site, although there is plenty of material to read.

Category: Science Fiction.
Contact: jackhammer@eggplant-productions.com
Editor: Raechel Henderson.
Publisher: Eggplant Productions.
Cost: Free.
Language: English.
ISSN: 1521-2602.
Payment: Payment is an initial $25 (US)-upon return of signed and dated contract-and 00.50c (US) for each day the story is posted on the website after an initial one month period.
Rights: First World Electronic Rights.
Reply Time: ASAP.

Guidelines and submission procedures:

Accepts speculative fiction stories up to 3,000 words. Stories are posted on the website for as long as readers vote for the story (no less than a month and no longer than a year).

Details: The editor is looking for speculative fiction up to 3,000 words, and her key criterion in evaluating a story is whether or not the story moves her in some way. Stories should have an element of speculation or the fantastic to them. The 3,000 word limit is firm.

Stories should be submitted as plain text email to submissions@eggplant-productions.com in the body of the message. No attachments. No snail mail submissions. Please include all pertinent information in the submission (see Email

Submission Standards for Eggplant Productions for more information). Please make sure that your email address is correct. Simultaneous submissions are accepted as long as they are disclosed as such in the submission.

No reprints. If the story has appeared anywhere in print, on the web, on a newsgroup or an emailed ezine, it is considered a reprint. The one exception to this is email-based critique groups (such as Critters). If the story has appeared on your web page (even if the only person who looked at it was your mother) it is still considered to be a reprint. If you have questions about these guidelines feel free to contact roach@eggplant-productions.com.

Kudzu (L)

www.etext.org/Zines/Kudzu

Kudzu was first published in 1994 in Oxford, Mississippi. Founded by Steven Jarvis and James E. Martin. Kudzu was originally planned to be a print literary journal, but lack of funds and an interest in the infant electronic publishing world led them to launch Kudzu electronically. The website has won quite a few awards. Provides a good selection of well-written fiction and poetry.

Category: Literary ezine.
Frequency: Quarterly.
Editor: W. Jarvis, publisher & editor-in-chief.
Contact: kudzu@etext.org.
Cost: Free.
Publisher: W. Jarvis.
Language: English.
Payment: Contact specific editor.
Rights: Contact specific editor - no previously published works (and that usually includes your own personal web site).
Reply Time: Contact specific editor.

Guidelines and submission procedures:

They look for good, solid, and professional writing. Kudzu accepts submissions from anyone and does not discriminate on any basis other than an admittedly subjective review of the work, not the author.

Fiction: They want short fiction (7,500 words or less) that is written well and tells a good story.
Essay: They are looking for strong writing that gets readers engaged in the subject. Personal essays, travelogues, humour, cultural or social commentary - style doesn't so much matter, as long as it's interesting, engaging, and well written.
How to submit: Submissions to Kudzu should be sent to the magazine via email. Files must be plain ASCII sent in the body of the email message. Do not send files

of any sort as attachments to your email. Please include a stable email address and a short bio. For those who do not have Internet email access, please contact the Editor for a snail mail address to which you can send snail mail submissions. All snail mail submissions should include: a hard copy printed neatly on white paper with generous margins (at least 1"), a self-addressed stamped envelope for replies, and an electronic copy of the submission on 3.5" floppy disk Email submissions and other correspondence to: kudzu@etext.org

Let's Live Magazine (NF)

http://www.letsliveonline.com

Let's Live has been going since 1933, and is considered to be America's foremost health and preventive health magazine reaching over 4 million readers. They are 90-95% freelance, which is good news for writers, and they actively encourage new writers to join their team. They have a good archive of material, which can be accessed by using the search facility on the archive page.

Category: Non fiction - lifestyle
Frequency: Updated regularly - see site for print details.
Circ: 1.5 million. (print)
Contact: info@letslivemag.com.
Editor: Beth Salmon
Cost: Free online version
Payment: Pays on acceptance.
Language: English
Rights: Buys first world rights with a 4-month embargo. No reprints.
Payment: Pays $700 for departments; $800-1000 for features.
Reply Time: 1 month.

Guidelines and submission procedures:

Writers with "intimate knowledge of natural health field. Able to meet deadlines and translate research into layman's terms." Articles run 1,200-2,000 words. Submit query and writing samples by mail with SAE. Query by email in the first instance.

Little Magazines
http://www.little-magazines.org.uk

Little Magazines is a directory of little magazines published in the UK and Ireland. It contains the names and addresses, subscription rates and submission guidelines of over 100 little magazines, making it the ideal resource for readers and writers everywhere. See below for examples of sites listed:

Amp Minizine - accepts photographs and artwork as well as prose
http://www.little-magazines.org.uk/a2z/a/amp.html

Head - thought-provoking non-fiction
http://www.little-magazines.org.uk/a2z/h/head.html

Rain Dog - welcomes contributions of original poetry
http://www.little-magazines.org.uk/a2z/r/rain_dog.html

Clicking on the link from the site will take you to a full listing, which will provide detailed information about guidelines and submission procedures.

littlemuch4women.com (L)

http://www.littlemuch4women.com

This website is all about the diversity in today's women writers. They run a monthly contest and submissions are always welcome. The categories include poetry, fiction or non-fiction, short stories, articles, book reviews, writer's tips, and the Editor's Choice. Just send them a Microsoft Word document of your work.

Category: Literary ezine.
Editor: Ken J. Davies, Thomas O. Holiday.
Contact: tholi52@concentric.net.
Cost: Free.
Publisher: Ken J. Davies.
Language: English.
Payment: Pays $5.00 per submission upon acceptance.
Rights: All copyrights will remain with the author and will be so noted with the work featured.
Reply Time: ASAP.

Guidelines and submission procedures:

Email Thomas O. Holiday for details: tholi52@concentric.net.

You may submit entries about any subject, done in any style. They are looking for quality writing. The length of the submission should be appropriate to the category. Let your story dictate its length. The preferred method of submission is in a Microsoft Word document. Send it as an attachment to email. Contact Thomas O. Holiday with your comments, suggestions or questions about this website.

millenniumSHIFT webzine (L)
http://www.millenniumshift.com

'You read it because it has a special quality. You write for it because you have a special flair. (Even brief exposure to our content can be addictive)…' millenniumSHIFT (Editor: Ken J. Davies).

Launched in 2000 this webzine has a distinct feel to it and a gutsy style to match. The editor doesn't expect writers to be politically correct, or mind them pushing out the boundaries in their writing, which is refreshing and certainly challenging. They are looking for writing that stirs the reader; gritty slices of life and irreverence seem to be the order of the day.

Category: Webzine.
Frequency: Updated regularly.
Editor: Ken J. Davies.
Contact: submit@millenniumshift.com.
Cost: Free.
Publisher: Hawkeye Studios.
Language: English.
Payment: $ 10.00 US for each item published (paid on the 15th day of the month following the posting).
Rights: Submissions, posted or otherwise, do not grant this publication any exclusivity, nor any rights beyond the right to post submitted items for the 30 day minimum period as stated.
Reply Time: Due to the volume of email, they may be able to respond only to those submissions selected for publication.

Guidelines and submission procedures:

'If you have something to say that's timely, compelling and has true character we welcome your submission — ideally under 800 words.'

Submission should be pasted into the body of an email. You may submit as often as you wish. Your posted item will include your by-line and a link to your email, and URL if available. Author's bio will not be included — All posted items will stand solely on their own merits.

Items accepted for publication will remain posted for a minimum of 30 days; after which either you or they may remove items; during which time you, the writer, will retain full copyrights to your material.

New Tribal Dawn Webzine (NF)
http://www.grailmedia.com/wz1/info/guidelines.html

New Tribal Dawn Webzine is devoted to the cultural heritage of indigenous peoples, and those whose common bond is that they are set apart from others in some way, such as Rastafarians or bikers. They are looking for articles that explore particular tribes, sub-cultures or social networks under the broad title of 'tribalism'. They are also interested in reviews, interviews of famous people, brief news items, and letters to the editor. Study of the content and style of the website is strongly advised.

Category: Webzine.
Frequency: Not listed.
Editor: David Bragi.
Contact: submissions@grailmedia.com.
Language: English.
Payment: They pay $50 per text article, upon acceptance. They do not pay for letters to the editor or brief news items.
Rights: All submissions must be previously unpublished online, except for brief news items. You must inform them if any part of your submission is already under copyright or in the public domain.
Reply Time: ASAP.

Guidelines and submission procedures:

They especially encourage submissions from minority or international contributors.

They prefer a length of 1,500 to 3,000 words; shorter for photo essays. Unpaid letters can be as short as you like. Check your facts. Nobody likes to receive five hundred emails stating that no, Reggae did not originate in Bermuda. If you identify a private individual (as opposed to a public figure) by name, or feature them prominently in a photograph, get their written permission before sending in the submission. They reserve the right to edit for content or length.

Format

All queries and manuscripts must be in text-only format. Do not send attachments; include the text in the body of the message. Query first if there are special HTML considerations (e.g. tables or graphics) or if you have photos.

Send all for-pay submissions to submissions@grailmedia.com.

Send all not-for-pay letters and news items to letters@grailmedia.com.

Send all other correspondence to info@grailmedia.com.

New Woman Online (NF)
www.newwomanonline.co.uk

New Woman Online, is the website of New Woman magazine. New Woman magazine supports women on the Internet by running as many Internet news items and features as possible. New Woman has launched this service in order to support female users by providing a unique place for women to browse for ideas, information and inspiration.

Category: Non fiction.
Frequency: Monthly.
Contact: Magazine Email: lollie.barr@ecm.emap.com
Editor: Jo Elvin.
Cost: 12 months - £28.80.
Web editor: Jackie Ryan.
Publisher: Dawn Bebe.
Language: English.
Payment: Query editor.
Rights: Query editor.
Reply time: ASAP.

Guidelines and submission procedures:

All enquiries about content should be made in the first instance to:
Editorial Co-ordinator: Lollie Barr
Email: lollie.barr@ecm.emap.com
Tel: 0171 437 9011
Fax: 0171 208 3585
Address: New Woman, Endeavour House, 189 Shaftsbury Avenue, London WC2H 8JG.

Please do not send unsolicited articles or photographs to New Woman magazine. Preliminary letters of enquiry should be addressed to the Editor of the relevant department and sent to New Woman Magazine, Endeavour House, 189

Shaftsbury Avenue, London WC2H 8JG. Letters should be sent via regular post.

New Woman has occasional work experience placements available. Requests for information should be sent via regular post to the Editor at New Woman, Endeavour House, 189 Shaftsbury Avenue, London WC2H 8JG.

Nocturne (L)
http://www.impure.org/myrrh

Nocturne claims to be a celebration of dark literature, artwork, and other forms of self-expression. The site is extremely impressive in terms of design, and the dark mood is certainly reflected in the writing that is published on the site. There is a clear statement indicating that some of the content may be offensive to certain individuals and not for the under 18's on the front page. So enter at your peril. They are looking for material that pushes the limits, and anything that explores new ground. The site includes a Writer's Forum, critiques and articles.

Category: Literary ezine.
Frequency: Weekly.
Contact: nocturne@poetic.com.
Editor: Mary Rajotte.
Cost: Free.
Language: English.
Payment: None.
Rights: Contact editor.
Reply Time: ASAP.

Guidelines and submission procedures:

They exclusively publish Horror Fiction and Dark Poetry, but are willing to make an exception for truly remarkable work in other dark genres.

Fiction: Though many publications put word limits on their submissions, they are willing to read longer pieces. However, due to web space, they reserve the right to serialise works and split them up between issues, if the need arises. They want to be frightened. Send them your most eerie, horrific writing. They are looking for writing that has a strong voice, dark undertones and intense conflict.

Poetry:

As with fiction, they are looking for unique voices and eloquent image-laden poetry, without being overdone. They want pieces that seduce the reader, that aren't forced into the mould of traditional ABAB rhyming schemes. If it doesn't work, don't submit it. Break free from the dull and routine, and strive toward new forms of expression.

Prose: Non-fiction submitted to the zine can deal with any topic. It doesn't necessarily have to have a dark theme, but still it must remain relevant to the theme of the site.

They will also accept pieces relating to the craft of writing. They are adding a section where other writers can gain knowledge on different techniques and information pertaining to the writing profession.

All submissions should be emailed to nocturne@poetic.com

You can submit your writing at any time. Instead of waiting months for a new issue of the zine, as traditional sites may do, the content at Nocturne is continually fresh. Material can appear on the site within two weeks.

All work should be submitted in one of the following manners to nocturne@poetic.com:

1.) Sent as a .txt or .rtf attachment
2.) Pasted into the body of an email

Note: Please specify the appropriate department to which you are submitting in the subject line of the email.

ALL work should include the following information:

A: Real name
B: Approx. word count
C: Email address
D: Title of story
E: Web page name and URL, if you would like them to link back to you
F: A short author's bio, containing past works, interests...whatever you would like to appear. Pics are also welcome.

Overland Express (NF)

www.overlandexpress.org/

An online journal of Australian writing. Overland Express considers new poetry and prose by Australian writers. The website is fairly impressive and the material published is of a very high standard. Read the editorial on site.

Category: Literary.
Frequency: Updated regularly.
Contact: overland@vu.edu.au.
Editor: Anna Hedigan, Tom Coverdale, Joel Magarey.
Cost: Free.
Language: English.
ISSN: 1444-3163.
Rights: Authors maintain all rights to their work.
Payment: Poems: $70; Prose: $100; Hypertext: $100.
Reply Time: ASAP.

Guidelines and submission procedures:

You can click on an email link at the website to submit directly.

Prose submissions should not exceed 2000 words per piece. Hypertext submissions should not exceed 2MB-file size. No simultaneous submissions. Provide a covering letter with contact details, including telephone number(s). If using a pseudonym, you must provide real name and contact details (not for publication). Prose submitted in hard copy should be 1.5-spaced; all other work, however er submitted, should be single-spaced.

Submission Formats:

Email to: overland@vu.edu.au. Electronic submissions should be sent as RTF (rich text format) attachments only. Do not send work in the body of an email. Include your covering letter (with contact details) in the body of your email. Enter the type of submission in the subject line: Poetry Submission, Fiction Submission, etc. Do not provide URLs to submit hypertext. Send your work as attachments, zipped if necessary, indicating the file type in the body of your email. Hypertext submissions using plug-ins should use Flaşh and Real Audio. Contact the editors before submitting work in other formats.

Post: Where possible the contact details in your covering letter should include an email address. Postal submissions received without an SAE may not be returned.

Post to: The Editors, overland express, 9 David Street, Footscray 3011, AUSTRALIA.

*Pif Magazine (L)
www.pifmagazine.com

PifMagazine.com has been ranked number sixteen in Writer's Digest's "50 Best Markets for Short Stories", who also commended Pif as "a showcase for quality poetry and short fiction by new and emerging writers." They seek original work from established and emerging fiction writers, poets, essayists, interviewers, and reviewers. Good comprehensive website but with an annoying banner across the bottom which can be quite distracting. Book review section. A recent issue of Pif included a review of some ezines, which made for interesting reading. Helps the writer keep an eye on what is happening on the internet.

Pif was founded in October of 1995 as a small fiction and poetry magazine with a circulation of around 500 readers. Since then it has become "The Starting Point for the Literary e-Press" and grown into three separate literary sites, Pif Magazine, Pilot-Search.com, and Zine-X.com. Pif currently has 75,000 original readers and 1 million impressions per month. The average reader returns to their sites 12.5 times per month.

Category: Literary.
Frequency: Monthly.
Editors: Camille Renshaw Senior Editor & Advertising Manager. camille@pifmagazine.com. Jen Bergmark Managing Editor & Fiction Editor
Language: English.
Rights: Contact editor.
Payment: Poetry (less than 100 lines) = $5 - $50 per poem. Short Stories (1,000 - 4,000 words) = $10-$50 per story. Micro Fiction (less than 500 words) = $5 - $50 per story. Commentary = $10-$50 per article. Review = $5-$50 per review.
Reply Time: ASAP.

Guidelines and submission procedures:

They accept all kinds of writing on an unsolicited basis. They only ask that you follow a few basic rules:
1. Get your submission to them by the issue deadline.

2. Always include a short bio with your submission.

3. Consideration of previously published works is at the discretion of the editor.

4. Snail mail submissions will not be considered.

Commentary: Editor Michael Burgin. Queries can be sent to Michael via email at michael@pifmagazine.com.

Poetry: Editor Anne Doolittle - anne@pifmagazine.com.

Fiction: Editor Jen Bergmark - jen@pifmagazine.com.

Issue Deadlines: The deadline for each issue is the 1st of the month prior to publication. Any submissions received after this date will be filed and not reviewed until the following month.

Word Length:

Micro Fiction = less than 1000 words in length

Macro Fiction = 1000 to 4000 words in length

Poetry = no line or word limit (but no more than 5 poems at once)

Reviews = 1000 to 2500 words

Interviews = 1200 to 3000 words

Essays = 1000 to 4000 words

Issue Themes: Email editors for details.

Pif Magazine only accepts electronic submissions. Snail mail submissions will not be accepted. They include an electronic form to fill out on the website. Email: Fiction: fiction@pifmagazine.com. Poetry: poetry@pifmagazine. Commentary/Reviews: commentary@pifmagazine.com. Letters to Editor: talkback@pifmagazine.com

Poetry.St Corner (G)
http://www.Poetry.St/

A weekly ezine showcasing poetry, prose, and verse via email. Every week you can receive the featured poem or verse that Poetry.St Corner showcases. Back issues are available on the site. Owned by the same group as Stark Raving Insanity.

Category: Literary/Poetry/Prose.
Frequency: Weekly ezine.
Audience: Readers of poetry, writers, and authors.
Contact: comments@Poetry.St.
Editor: Carla Radwanski.
Publisher: H. Roger Baker II.
Cost: Free.
Language: English.
Rights: By submitting the work, the author gives permission to Digital
Images Publishing Studios to publish the work in Poetry.St Corner. However, the author maintains the copyright for the work.
Payment: Currently, Poetry.St Corner does not pay contributors. However, the author maintains the copyright for the work and will receive space for their bio.
Reply time: Poetry.St Corner will attempt to respond within 30 days.

Guidelines and submission procedures:

Well-crafted poetry, prose, or verse. Previously published works are accepted. Submissions are not to exceed 60 lines. They place no restrictions on subject matter or form. However, pieces containing excessive use of adult language and/or adult subject matter will not be considered.

Poetry.St Corner currently accepts only email submissions. Submit your work to the email address: submit@Poetry.St, with "PSC submission" in the subject line. Do not send attachments. Submissions with attachments will be deleted immediately, unopened and unread. Include your name, address, city, state, zip code, and title of the work and a 100 word or less bio. Email: comments@Poetry.St

Postal Mail: Poetry.St Corner, Digital Images Publishing Studios, P O Box 44894, Columbus, Ohio 43204, USA.

*Quantum Muse (G)

www.quantummuse.com

They are committed to providing aspiring writers and artists with a free and open forum for expression. They state on the front page of the site that their goal is *"to provide the discriminating reader with the best fiction we can obtain without spending any of our beer money."* A Quantum Muse anthology "Quantum Musings" is available.

Category: Science Fiction, Fantasy, and Alternative.
Frequency: Updated regularly.
Contact: editors@quantummuse.com
Editor: Michael Gallant, Raymond Coulombe, Timothy O. Goyette.
Artist/Graphic Designer: Rebecca Kemp (Gallant).
Cost: $11.95 for anthology.
Language: English.
Rights: All copyrights to your story and/or artwork belong to you.
Payment: None.
Reply Time: ASAP.

Guidelines and submission procedures:

They have an 8,000-word limit. You may submit longer works if they can be serialised. Serialised works have special guidelines. They prefer electronic submissions. Simply save your work as ASCII text (plain text with paragraph breaks) and be prepared to paste it into either a form (preferred) or an email.

For artwork, again submitting electronically is best. Send them your website address.

If you do not have a website, please send two or three images in .JPEG or .GIF format only via email attachment. Each piece must be less than 100k. You can also send your work on disk using the same format. Give a brief informative blurb on each piece, such as title, medium, size and whether it's for sale. Include a short bio for yourself as well. A paragraph will do or use their form.

Quill (NF)
http://www.spj.org

The official publication of the Society of Professional Journalists and the Sigma Delta Chi Foundation. In addition to news about SPJ and the Foundation, the magazine examines issues of interest to working journalists and editors. Welcomes new writers, "but they must show exceptional promise, as we do not have the wherewithal to hold hands!" They require extremely well-researched material that will be of keen interest to working print and broadcast journalists, editors and news directors, publishers and the world of journalism academe. They do not publish opinion pieces or commentary from freelance contributors. Website 60% freelance.

Category: Non fiction/journalism.
Frequency: 10 issues/year.
Circ: 15K.
Contact: jmohl@spjhq.org.
Editor: Jeff Mohl.
Cost: Subscriptions: $29. $50 outside US.
Language: English/Italian.
Rights: Buys first world rights. Rarely accepts reprints.
Payment: Pays from $100 for short pieces to $1,200 for major cover articles. Pays on publication. Publishes ms 2-3 months after acceptance.
Reply Time: ASAP.

Guidelines and submission procedures:

Guidelines at website (click on Quill, then Story Submissions). Prefers to assign stories rather than accept random submissions. Submit resume and clips to Query Editor.

Photos/Art: Digital art required; payment varies.

Richmond Review (L)

http://www.richmondreview.co.uk

The Richmond Review was established in October 1995 as the UK's first literary magazine to be published exclusively on the World Wide Web. Updated at least monthly, the magazine has a team of around twenty-five regular contributors and editors, many of whom work in London book publishing. The site is very informative, including interviews, book reviews, features and essays on a variety of subjects that will interest writers. Should interest those with an eclectic mix of tastes. Provides a list of FAQ's that should answer any query about submitting material.

Category: Literary.
Frequency: Monthly.
Editor: Geoff Mulligan.
Contact: editor@richmondreview.co.uk.
Publisher: The Richmond Review is produced by Steven Kelly.
Cost: Free.
Language: English.
Payment: Occasionally.
Rights: They typically ask for a non-exclusive license from their contributors, allowing them to publish the work for a limited term. The original authors own almost all copyrights.
Reply Time: Months.

Guidelines and submission procedures:

No poetry. If you want to review some books for them, take a look at some of their reviews and send in a few samples of your work. Reviews should normally be between 300-500 words.

Stories: Send one or two short stories by email to the editor (plain text or HTML only, please - anything else won't get read for reasons of security and/or compatibility). Email an outline of your idea for any article to the editor with some brief biographical information. Use the single word "Submission" in the subject line of your message.

Geoff Mulligan Editor-at-Large in London: geoff.mulligan@richmondreview.co.uk

Sara Rance Reviews Editor: sara.rance@richmondreview.co.uk

Jason Starr New York editor: jason.starr@richmondreview.co.uk

Liz Rowlinson Features editor: liz.rowlinson@richmondreview.co.uk

Jon Mitchell Crime Reporter: ajon.mitchell@richmondreview.co.uk

Polly Rance Philosophy Editor: polly.rance@richmondreview.co.uk

Helena Mary Smith Travel Editor: helena.smith@richmondreview.co.uk

Michael Bradshaw Poetry Editor: michael.bradshaw@richmondreview.co.uk

SageBase (CP)
http://www.sagebase.com

SageBase is a place where your articles can be viewed. They pay writers based on click through percentages rather than a flat fee or by word. You have to become a 'Sage' to contribute, but it is a good example of a number of sites that fall into this general category. They are, however, only interested in well written, quality material.

Category: Non-fiction.
Contact: info@SageBase.com.
Editor: Tammy Mackenzie - editor@SageBase.com.
Language: English.
Rights: Query editor.
Payment: 50% of revenue generated by their banner ads or book sales on the page your article is showcased on.
Reply Time: All messages will be read, and replies will be sent as promptly as possible.

Guidelines and submission procedures:

Non-fiction articles 200-1000 words (all topics). Articles must be timeless with a how-to focus (i.e. no "event" articles).

Contact individual Sages: (Please include the name of the Sage in the subject line.)
sages@SageBase.com

You can earn bonuses for writing the Featured Article of the Week. As your Sage experience grows, you'll be assigned articles and paid for them on the spot. You can also credit your publication on SageBase to other editors to get new assignments, featured articles and columns.

Salon Magazine (NF)
www.salon.com

Salon.com is an Internet media company that produces a network of 11 original content sites and hosts MP3Lit.com, a digital audio literature site, as well as two online communities — Table Talk and The WELL. The content sites include News, Politics2000, Technology, Arts & Entertainment, Business, Health, Books, Sex, Mothers Who Think, People and Comics, and are updated daily or more frequently. Salon.com also maintains an e-commerce gateway, Salon Shop, which showcases Salon.com staff reviews and recommendations on a wide range of consumer goods plus information on the latest products from affiliated merchants and partners.

Category: Non-fiction.
Frequency: Updated regularly.
Contact: dtalbot@salon.com.
Editor: David Talbot.
Cost: Free.
Language: English.
Rights: Query editor.
Payments: Query editor.
Reply Time: If you have not heard back from them, after three weeks, assume that they will not be able to use your idea or submission.

Guidelines and submission procedures:

Salon welcomes article queries and submissions. The best way to submit articles and story pitches is via email. They ask that you send the text of your query or submission in plain text in the body of your email, rather than as an attached file, as they may not be able to read the format of your file.

If you wish to contribute, please spend some time familiarising yourself with Salon's various sites and features. Put the words "EDITORIAL SUBMISSIONS" in the subject line of the email. You can find the appropriate editor's name on Salon's Staff page. Tell them about yourself: your experience and background as a writer and qualifications for writing a particular story. If you have clips you can send them via email, or Web addresses of pages that contain your work. Send them a representative sampling (no more than three or four).

SilverKris (NF)
www.singaporeair.com

The in-flight magazine of Singapore Airlines. This may seem like a peculiar choice but there are a lot of airlines out there with in-flight magazines looking for good material to include in their publications.

Category: Non-fiction.
Frequency: Monthly.
Editor: Steve Thompson, Group Editor.
Contact: silverkris@ mph.com.sg
Cost: Free.
Publisher: SIA by MPH Magazines (S) Pte Ltd.
Language: English/Chinese-language section.
Payment: Basic rates are S$250 per 1,000 published words. Payment for photos depends on published size - S$200 for double-page spread or less, S$100 for full page or less, S$75 for half page or less, S$50 for quarter page or less, S$250 for cover. Photo essays are paid at a flat rate, regardless of the number of photos used - S$1,000 for four pages, S$1,250 for six pages and S$1,500 for eight pages.
Rights: They ask for first in-flight and first Asian rights in both text and photos.
Reply Time: ASAP.

Guidelines and submission procedures:

They feature travel and adventure stories - mostly related to SIA destinations - but also articles on well known personalities, food and beverage, the arts and collectables, history and archaeology, sports and pastimes, ecology and the environment, business and finance, science and technology, and humour.
The style should be entertaining, but also knowledgeable and informative.

Avoid: A guide-book approach. Issues: political, racial, religious or whatever - that might offend a sensitive reader. Any mention of airlines competing with SIA. Giving free advertising to commercial establishments or SIA's competitors. Any mention of death, air crashes or sex.

Stories can range up to 2,000 words in length and should be accompanied by 30-40 high-quality original captioned colour transparencies. They publish a four- , six- or eight-page photo essay each month: submit 50-60 original captioned transparencies, together with an introductory text of 500 words or so. Please do not submit transparencies with a date imprinted on them. Short, back-of-the-book features are also acceptable, and no photos are required for these.

Please include a brief note on yourself - who you are, where you live, what kind of writing or photography you do, any major publications your work has been published in. Please send text in electronic form - either by email or on diskette in "text only" format. Transparencies and two copies of the relevant issue will be sent to the contributor by registered airmail on publication. Please note that, due to the large amount of material on hand, it may take some time for a story to appear in print.

SilverKris, 12 Tagore Drive, Singapore 787621. P(65)4538200. F(65)4538600

Slope (G)
www.slope.org

Slope is a bi-monthly online journal devoted to worldwide contemporary poetry in English. They encourage new and emerging writers, but frequently publish award-winning and established poets. Slope occasionally features "sampler" issues. Recent examples include New Avant Poetry (Issue 5), Contemporary Women's Poetry (Issue 6) and New Welsh and British Poetry (Issue 9). The website is a bit scrappy on information, hence lack of contact details. But visit the site and see if you can find an email address. They plan to produce a print version of their collection of poetry.

Category: Poetry.
Frequency: Bi-monthly.
Contact:
Editor: Ethan Paquin.
Cost: Free.
Language: English.
Rights: Rights revert to poets upon publication.
Payment: Non paying, non-profit Ezine.
Reply Time: ASAP.

Guidelines and submission procedures:

The editor invites electronic submissions of 2 to 6 poems in experimental and traditional styles. All poems submitted must be previously unpublished and accompanied by a brief biographical note. Unsolicited poems, reviews, interviews and poems in translation will be considered year-round. Please query before sending reviews and interviews.

Spike (NF)
www.spikemagazine.com

Spike is about people, books and ideas. First arriving online in June 1996, Spike continues to update on a frequent but erratic basis, publishing interviews, features, reviews and new writing, both by established and unpublished authors. Spike features not only the famous and the up and coming but the totally obscure too - in short; whatever they think is worthwhile. Despite its dot.com address, Spike is wholly based in the UK. All of Spike's contributors, including the editor, have progressed from writing for Spike for free, to writing for good money in the traditional media.

Category: New Writing.
Frequency: Updated regularly.
Contact: chris@spikemagazine.com.
Editor: Chris Mitchell.
Cost: Free.
Language: English.
Rights: Query editor.
Payment: None. Spike is run for fun, not profit.
Reply Time: ASAP.

Guidelines and submission procedures:

Send them an outline of what you want to contribute to chris@spikemagazine.com. Book reviews should be no longer than 700 words and interviews and features no longer than 2,000 words. They don't generally like poetry, so if you do submit it, make sure it is good. They are also interested in features and interviews with bands, as well as exceptionally written album and gig reviews. They are also happy to publish articles that have appeared elsewhere in print (i.e. not on the Internet).

*Stark Raving Sanity (L)
http://www.stormloader.com/dips/

Stark Raving Sanity is an electronic literary journal showcasing anything literary, artistic, or interesting. This includes poems, short stories, theoretical works and critical essays. It goes without saying that they are looking for completely original and offbeat pieces. Study the website with care before submitting material and follow their guidelines. The site provides good details about submission procedures, what they are about, and who to submit material to.

Category: Electronic Literary Journal.
Frequency: Semi-annual.
Contact: comments@StarkRavingSanity.com.
Editor: Mike S. DuBose.
Publisher: Roger Baker II.
Cost: Free.
Language: English.
ISSN: 1091-7357.
Rights: Stark Raving Sanity acquires one-time electronic publication rights to all accepted works. No previously published works will be accepted. Upon publication, all rights revert back to the author. Once a work has appeared in SRS, the author may republish the work elsewhere. However, please provide credit to Stark Raving Sanity.
Payment: At this time SRS cannot pay its contributors. However, the authors submitted bio will be published.
Reply Time: SRS will attempt to reply within 120 days.

Guidelines and submission procedures:

All pieces must not have been previously published and cannot be a simultaneous submission.

Poetry: Verse or prose poems accepted. While pieces relating to any topic or theme are acceptable, remember SRS looks for original and somewhat offbeat pieces. There is no true length limit, but please refrain from pieces exceeding 20 pages.

Fiction: Fiction works should be well crafted, cutting edge, off the wall, eclectic, and most importantly original. Pieces should not exceed 20 pages and should be submitted in standard format.

Non-fiction: Non-fiction pieces should be well-written and original pieces. Things such as critical essays and theoretical works are acceptable. Pieces can be based on any theme or topic and cannot exceed 20 pages.

Artwork: Looking for cover art. Artwork should be sent as JPEG or GIF files. It should stay true to the ideas presented by SRS (offbeat, eclectic, etc.) and should be original work.

Submissions are preferred via email with the work within the body of the email message. However, attachments, such as Word 6.0 (.doc) or text (.txt) are accepted as well. Also, submissions can be sent by postal mail as hard copy works or on disk (to have your disk returned a SAE must be included). All submissions must include a bio containing the author's name, address, city, state, zip code, email address and the title of the work. Email: submit@StarkRavingSanity.com, with "SRS submission" in the subject line.

Postal Mail: Stark Raving Sanity, Submissions, Digital Images Publishing Studios,

P O Box 44894, Columbus, Ohio 43204, USA.

The Charlotte Austin Review - formerly The Quill (L)
www.charlotteaustinreviewltd.com

The Charlotte Austin Review Ltd is primarily an extensive book review site, with reviews presented in a number of categories. All reviewers are fully profiled and make up a growing team of 22 reviewers and editors. The site also publishes interviews with authors and publishers, selected short fiction from emerging writers, and Reflections, thoughts on the writing life from published authors.

Category: Literary Reviews.
Frequency: Updated regularly.
Contact: editor@charlotteaustinreviewltd.com.
Editor: Charlotte Austin.
Cost: Free.
Language: English.
Rights: Contact Editor.
Payment: There is no payment offered at this time for submissions.
Reply Time: ASAP.
Hits: Site statistics recorded from Feb. 1/2000 to August 31/2000 show a total of 425,000.

Guidelines and submission procedures:

They welcome contributions, sent as email or as MS Word attachment only.

In selecting material for publication, they look for conciseness and effective use of language. Contributions are acknowledged with a by-line, bio and photo as applicable.

Book Reviews: All reviews are written by a team of regular reviewers. To be considered as a possible reviewer, email the editor with a sample of your work.
Columns: All columns are written by regular columnists and are published to answer a variety of questions from readers. To suggest a column, email the editor with a precise proposal and a plan for an on-going column.

Features: Features include interviews or conversations with authors and publishers, and what editors and publishers look for.

Reflections: Thoughts and true inspirational stories on the writing life from published authors.

Short Fiction: Length 1,500 - 6,000 words. Preferred: 2,500 words. No children's stories, easy readers, picture books and essays. They look for well-crafted, traditional short stories with depth and meaning.

The Charlotte Austin Review can accept submissions year round. New mailing address is: 3364 BobWhite Mews, Mississauga, Ontario L5N 6E7, Canada.

*The Edge (L)
www.users.globalnet.co.uk/~houghtong/index.htm

The Edge publishes fiction, features, and interviews, book, film, video, sound-track & graphic novel reviews and comment columns. Has included new fiction by Steve Beard, Eric Brown, Michael Moorcock and Peter Whitehead; extensive interviews with Caitlin R Kiernan and Anthony Frewin; Iain Sinclair on London, Peter Ackroyd and Michael Moorcock. Read the editorial posted by Graham Evans on the site to get a clearer picture, and understanding, of what The Edge is all about before you submit material to them. "The Edge is for people who like their entertainment a little more sophisticated than the latest on Bill and Monica, and their exchanges of cute frog mugs and books with titles like Oy Vey: What They Say, A Guide To Jewish Slang."

Category: Literary Publication.
Contact: houghtong@globalnet.co.uk.
Editor: Graham Evans.
Cost: UK, current issue: £2.95 per issue; next issue, £3.50.
Language: English.
Rights: First Publication Rights (in any media, anywhere in the world) only.
Payment: Payments are negotiable (up to £65 per 1000 words). Payment is made on publication, and they will send you the proofs before printing.
Reply Time: Three weeks.

Guidelines and submission procedures:

Please read carefully and look at the magazine before contacting them.

The Edge is interested in fiction, features and reviews by writers from any-where in the world. Please address to Graham Evans. They do not read submissions sent by email. Please note that The Edge accepts no responsibility for unsolicited submissions, and does not suffer fools gladly.

Fiction:
The Edge publishes unusual, interesting short stories of any length (not whole

novels or sequels to work published elsewhere). Many have urban themes, and/or could be described (by others) as modern and borderline gothic horror/fantasy/SF, 'slipstream' fiction, crime fiction or erotica; please don't send clichéd stories. Experimental work is welcome. There is always room for new names. A lot of their fiction has subsequently been collected into book form. The Edge is, obviously, read by many professional writers and editors. Please send one story at a time, and don't email fiction to them.

Non-fiction:
Features, including interviews, are usually commissioned. These are from 2-20,000 words. Please write with a sample of your work, published or unpublished, with appropriate return postage (see below) unless you are enclosing your email address.

They have never published an unsolicited review. Those interested in book or film reviewing should look at a copy of the magazine and send examples of their work (published or unpublished).

Artwork:
Illustrators, cover artists and cartoonists are not required. Comic strip submissions will be considered, either serious or humorous, but look at the magazine (not just the site) first. They look at either complete strips or stories, or sample pages. All artwork sent must be disposable.

Requirements:
Please type double-spaced, number the pages of typescripts, and include your name and address and the approximate word-length. Paperclip or staple your work. Oddly (it seems) we mean all this, including the last bit. No poetry, simultaneous submissions or submissions by email or on disk.

*The Fiction Writer (L)
www.thefictionwriter.com

Very professional looking website with good resources and links for writers. Short fiction competition, online store and free email services, message board and chat.

Category: Literary.
Frequency: Updated regularly.
Contact: submissions@thefictionwriter.com.
Editor: Joyce Siedler, Managing Editor. Jeanne E. Fredriksen, Copy Editor.
Cost: Free.
Language: English.
Rights: First-time, exclusive rights to publish your article on The Fiction Writer site for one year. Non-exclusive rights after the first year (you are free to sell your article elsewhere).
Payment: $50.
Reply Time: ASAP.

Guidelines and submission procedures:

The Fiction Writer: Online Literary Magazine will consider submissions from all writers, regardless of experience.

Do not send attachments. Include the piece in the body of the email. Submit the piece single-spaced with a blank line between paragraphs. Include your name, title of the piece, writing experience if any, and the piece. If you cite URL's in the article, please include the 'http://' to make it easy for readers to link to the site.

Submissions that do not adhere to these guidelines will be returned unread.

Non-fiction - No simultaneous submissions: 1000 - 3500 words.

These should be non-fiction articles about the craft of writing fiction. They are looking for articles on topics such as market tips, submission advice, interviews, and technique tips and tricks. They like a journalistic, matter of fact style for non-fiction. Send the finished piece to submissions@thefictionwriter.com. Include your name, writing experience if any, the title of the piece, and the piece in the body of the email.

Short story/essay - No simultaneous submissions: 1500-5000 words.

Some acceptable categories are romance, science fiction, speculative fiction, mysteries, and historical fiction. Send the finished piece to submissions@thefictionwriter.com. Include your name, writing experience if any, the title of the piece, and your piece in the body of the email.

*The Mystery Review (G)
www.inline-online.com/mystery/

A quarterly publication for mystery readers. Includes book reviews, interviews with authors and those related to the mystery/suspense genre, thematic articles, and mystery fiction, bookstore profiles, word games and puzzles, and information about new releases. 95% freelance. Prefers to work with previously published writers. The website has a distinctive feel to it and there is some nice artwork on the covers of the publication. They don't archive past publications in their entirety but they do provide a good overview of the contents. This is a quality quarterly that publishes distinctive, well-written material.

Category: Mystery.
Frequency: Quarterly.
Circ: 6,500.
Contact: mystrev@reach.net.
Editor: Barbara Davey.
Publisher:
Cost: Subscription $20 in the United States; $21.50 (CDN includes GST) in Canada; $28 (US) elsewhere.
Language: English.
Rights: Purchases First Rights. No reprints.
Payment: By-line and cash honorarium for materials accepted. Honorarium paid on publication.
Reply Time: Response time 3-4 weeks. Publishes ms approx. 6-9 months after acceptance.

Guidelines and submission procedures:

Looking for author interviews, thematic articles. Article length depends on article type. Query the editor with topic contemplated. Query, with photocopies of previously published articles.

Photos/Art: Line illustrations used for cover and inside articles. HINTS: Check out the guidelines on their website.

Interviews: authors or others related to the mystery genre (editors, law enforcement personnel, etc.) *range from 2,000 to 5,000 words, depending on subject * require photos and/or other illustrations, which can be reproduced in black ink

Truly Mysterious: * "real life" unsolved mysteries - historical or contemporary * 2,000 to 5,000 words * photos/ illustrations required

Book Reviews: * Query with photocopies of your published reviews * 500 to 700 words (1 to 1 1/2 typewritten pages)

Book Shop Beat: * approximately 500 words * b/w photo of store, proprietor, business logotype, etc. required questionnaire covering basic information required available from the editor

Other Articles: Got an idea for a thematic piece or other mystery related article? They're always open to suggestions – please query.

Trivia, Puzzles, Shorts short filler articles, puzzles and word games related to the mystery/suspense genre

Illustrations: * Black and white cover illustrations and article illustrations are assigned. Query with samples of your work.

The Rue Bella (L)
www.ruebella.co.uk

Rue Bella a short story and poetry magazine set up in 1998 and currently in its 5th volume. They offer a place for unestablished writers to rub shoulders with leading international names, such as Benjamin Zephaniah, Brian Patten and Ed Mycue. The site is a bit patchy on details for submissions and simply states that submissions should be sent to an email address. In fact the site in general lacks information, although having a name like Benjamin Zephaniah on the front page makes up for any failings.

Category: Literary.
Contact: editors@ruebella.co.uk
Editor: Nigel and Geoff Bird.
Cost: £3.00.
Language: English.
Rights: No rights.
Payment: One free copy.
Reply Time: ASAP.
Circ. 300-400.

Guidelines and submission procedures:

They are mostly interested in providing a voice and some encouragement for new writers. Their submission details are straightforward - send them your work and they'll do their best.

The Write Moves (NF)

http://www.geocities.com/allthewritemoves2000/

All the Write Moves provides up-to-date information about the craft of writing for the web and finding freelance internet writing resources for freelance web writers. They accept articles on any aspect of web writing and publishing. These may include how-to, marketing, research techniques, or anything else pertaining to freelance web writing.

Category: Non fiction.
Contact: kal_1@msn.com.
Editor: Not listed.
Frequency: Bi-weekly.
Cost: Free for freelance writers.
Language: English.
Rights: They buy first electronic rights and archive rights. Please let them know if you are submitting a reprint. You may republish your article after it has appeared in The Write Moves.
Payment: Payment is $10 upon acceptance.
Reply Time: ASAP.

Guidelines and submission procedures:

Articles should be from 800-1000 words in length. Check the newsletter first to see if they have already published an article on your topic.

If your work is accepted, it will run in the newsletter and on the Feature Articles page on the website for one month. If you choose, you may also post on the website your bio and pic, as well as any links to other writing samples you have and/or your web page.

They will do minor editing, if needed, but nothing more. They will check with you if any changes need to be made to your article before they run it. There will be a separate page for each author.

Query first. Your query should consist of a well thought-out outline of the points you intend to cover in your article. Please do not query with a general idea or ask for an assignment. Please send your query with WRITE MOVES QUERY in the subject line of your email.

The Writer's Block Emagazine (NF)

http://emily_bivens.homestead.com/wbemagazine.html

This emagazine is a bit lightweight compared to other ezines, although there are some interesting articles to be found. They are also seeking material for their new emagazine, The Toy Box, on the subjects of Pregnancy, Infants, Toddlers and Teenagers.

Category: Non-fiction.
Contact: emily_bivens@excite.com.
Editor: Emily Bivens.
Cost: Free.
Language: English.
Rights: They buy no rights. This way you can make the most money for your writing.
Payment: They pay $5 per piece upon publication.
Reply Time: ASAP.

Guidelines and submission procedures:

They accept the following genres of writing: non-fiction, fiction, short story, novel excerpts, poetry, horror, science fiction, fantasy, romance, personal experience essays. If you have something you feel fits in another category, contact them to see if it is material they accept. You do not need to query. Simply send your submission in the body of an email. No attachments. Word length: 1500 words maximum

*Web del Sol (L)

www.webdelsol.com

The subtitle for Web del Sol is 'The Eclectic Culture System' and the site certainly lives up to expectations. It is more a way of life than a website and you will want to return again and again.

WDS is a collaboration on the part of dozens of dedicated, volunteer editors, writers, poets, artists, and staff whose job it is to acquire and frame the finest contemporary literary art and culture available in America and abroad, and to array it in such a manner that it speaks for itself. The purpose of WDS is therefore multi-fold. WDS exists to: Explore, promote, and create new forms of artistic and literary expression in new media, hypertext, photography, and the literary arts, and to build an electronic community and nexus, which fosters collaboration between these forms. Create and sustain a new genre of film known as "literary arts film." WDS obtains and promotes collaboration between the independent film community and the literary arts community of writers through its Literary Arts Film Project. Promote, fund, and support the writing, publishing, and reading of contemporary literature in electronic media. Includes 5_Trope, In Posse Review, and La Petite Zine

Category: Literary ezines.
Frequency: Updated regularly.
Editor: Michael Neff.
Contact: editor@webdelsol.com.
Cost: Free.
Language: English.
Payment: Query individual ezine.
Rights: Once work is accepted for publication, Web Del Sol acquires the rights to publish. After publication, rights revert to the contributor. Contributor agrees, however, that any subsequent publication, whether in print or on the web, must acknowledge Web Del Sol. By contributing, you affirm that you have read and agree with the submission guidelines on this page. Query individual editors for other ezines.
Reply Time: Depends on publication.

Guidelines and submission procedures:

Editor's Picks at Web Del Sol seeks to publish 'poetry, prose poetry, short stories, flash fiction, creative non-fiction, quiction, and essays.' All forms and styles are considered, the exception being genre fiction. Editors look for work, which builds on unique content and subject matter.

Work should reside in the body of the mail, or attached as Word 6 or .rtf file (Rich Text Format). If necessary, italics may be indicated by use of the following characters: [i]...[/i]. Due to limited staff time, the editor asks that contributors please proof submissions carefully before submitting.

NOTE: For those editors who do not own Macs, any Mac files attached to mails cannot be opened unless first converted to pc-IBM format prior to mailing.

Trope:

Extraordinary and "bleeding edge" fiction, poetry, and hybrid forms. Before you submit work to 5_Trope, have a look at the work on exhibit in their current and previous issues - and you'll discover that what they are seeking is the innovative and the unprecedented. They are not keen on pieces which obviously derive from structured writing programmes or workshops.

Guidelines for Submission:

1. Don't bluff your way out of your heart, but deliver the thing itself on the page.
2. Don't just speak the language— make the language speak you.
3. Choose topics, people, situations, etc. not usually examined by the literary lens; or else depict the commonplace using uncommon means: a unique style, angle, or approach. (And they prefer that you present your submission within the body of an email. Please include a concise autobiographical statement. Also, because of the limited number of writers appearing in each issue and their editorial mission to feature the unexampled and the unpredictable, contributors are sure to understand that 5_Trope will rarely publish any one writer more than once a year. Your submission should be addressed to Editor Joan Howard: 5Trope@webdelsol.com.)

In Posse Review:

Publishes solid fiction, short-shorts, prose poetry, and plans to publish poetry also.

Submissions:

In Posse accepts submissions via the Internet. of original works less than 3500 words. No simultaneous submissions. Stories should be included in the body of the email if possible, if not, please explain why. Submissions will not be accepted through regular mail. Contact Editor Rachel Callaghan for additional details. In Posse is granted exclusive electronic rights for a period of 120 days. Author retains right to publish work in non-electronic form at any time. Works will also be archived online. Writers are encouraged to submit classic short fiction as well as short-shorts, prose poetry, poetry, micro-shorts, flash fictions, and other hybrid fiction forms. They are also interested in creative non-fiction, including literary memoir. Innovation is encouraged. Submissions are accepted year round. Unfortunately, there is no remuneration.

La Petite Zine:

Poetry of the east and west, emphasis on skill, short works of fiction also, articles, scripts.

Submissions: La Petite Zine looks for excellent poetry, fiction, articles, and scripts. We acquire First Rights or one-time rights. You retain the copyright. Please send no previously published work (either print or online), and if the work is accepted anywhere else after you have sent it to them, they request you drop them a line withdrawing it from consideration. There is no monetary compensation at this time. Submissions of tanka, sijo, ghazals, or haibun for the East Bank should be sent to Tom Hartman. Poetry submissions for West Bank poetry, fiction, along with queries for articles, short scripts, and other media should be sent to Daniel M. Nester.

They accept email submissions only, with pieces pasted as plain text in the body of the message. A short writerly bio (50 words or less) is a good idea as well. They require that you put in your email subject line the following information:

LPZ.lastname.genre.date ...with the date being a month-date-year format.

This submission, for instance, came from a person with the surname Keats, who will send poetry to LPZ on July 4th, 2037—LPZ.keats.poetry.7.4.2037. This nifty system ensures efficient filing for editors and authors alike. They encourage compliance. They suggest 3-5 poems max, essays and fiction of under 2000 words, Allow 1-2 months for them to get back to you. Email your submissions to lapetite@webdelsol.com. Email East Bank submissions to the East Bank editor.

Flashpoint: where the arts and politics clash. Publishes poetry (including language poetry), fiction, experimental forms, and provocative essays. Also open to photography exhibits. High quality work only.

Wild and Whirling Words (L)
www.wildandwhirlingwords.com

Wild and Whirling Words encourages writers to speak their minds and express the creative side in their submissions. They publish material just as it is sent to them so beware; they make no apology for material that does appear on the site. "The works that are linked to from this page were not written by any member of Wild and Whirling Word's staff and do not necessarily express the views of Wild and Whirling Words." This site comes by way of a good contrast to sites like The Edge. Study each of them carefully and form your own opinion.

Category: Literary ezine.
Frequency: Updated regularly.
Contact: editor@wildandwhirlingwords.com.
Editor: Joshua Steen.
Cost: Free.
Language: English.
Rights: They will not claim any rights to your works, with the exception that you allow them to post your work on the site.
Payment: Currently, Wild and Whirling Words does not pay contributors.
Reply time: ASAP.

Guidelines and submission procedures:

Online submission form. It is not necessary to enter any personal information, although all information regarding the work to be submitted is required. They recommended that you fill in as many elements as possible so that you can be contacted if there is a problem or question concerning your work. They do not give out any of the information and will not send you any unsolicited email. Only the editorial staff will see your personal details, but your name, if included, will appear with your work when posted. If you do not include your name your work will be displayed as "by Anonymous".

World Wide Freelance Writer (NF)
www.worldwidefreelance.com

This site is dedicated to informing writers of international freelance writing markets, particularly those outside North America. Although they are a paying market, their rate per article is currently quite low but as the site grows they say they will offer increasingly attractive fees and writers who have already contributed will have an excellent opportunity to sell further pieces.

Category: Freelance.
Frequency: Updated regularly.
Contact: editor@worldwidefreelance.com
Editor: Gary McLaren.
Cost: Free.
Language: English.
Rights: If they accept your article they purchase: website: - non-exclusive rights to publish your article on Worldwide Freelance Writer website, and Newsletter: - one-time non-exclusive world wide rights to print your article in Worldwide Freelance Writer electronic newsletter and the non-exclusive right to reprint your work in archival versions of our newsletter.
Payment: The current fee is HK$160 (Hong Kong Dollars) (approx. US$20) per article, upon publication.
Reply Time: ASAP.

Guidelines and submission procedures:

Reprints are OK. If your article has appeared elsewhere, please tell them where. Preferred article length is around 800-1000 words. All queries and articles must be submitted by email in the body of the message (no attachments). Send to editor@worldwidefreelance.com, with "Submissions" as the subject. They only accept email submissions, so do not post hard copies of your manuscript. They will not be returned. They are looking for articles on: how to write for international markets, how to successfully sell writing to international markets success stories and related topics. Email the Editor for current requirements.

Writer Online (NF)

http://www.novalearn.com/wol

Writer Online is a free newsletter/ezine for writers of all kinds, from novelists and playwrights to technical and multimedia writers. Circulation is growing rapidly and is now nearing 35,000. They also produce Writer Online Marketplace, a sister publication to Writer Online. They are always looking for volunteer writers. Volunteer contributions will carry the author's by-line and could lead to a staff position. Email for more information.

Category: Fiction/Non-Fiction.
Frequency: Weekly.
Circ: 35,000.
Contact: creosote1@hotmail.com.
Editor: T. M. Wright.
Publisher: Terry Boothman.
Cost: Free.
Language: English.
ISSN: None.
Rights: First/second.
Payment: Poetry $1.00 per line. Fiction/Non-fiction 5-10c per word. Reprints $20.00.
Reply Time: Allow up to four weeks.

Guidelines and submission procedures:

Non-fiction: Articles should address the craft, marketing, or publishing of writing. They prefer articles that offer examples, and use direct quotes from credible sources such as books, papers, addresses and URLs where readers can obtain further information.

Payment is 5 -10 cents a word upon publication.

Fiction: Writer Online is looking for quality fiction, in all genres. Fiction of all kinds up to 1,200 words. They do accept "flash fiction" (50 to 200 words), though this is probably the toughest area for new writers to break into. Payment for fiction is from 5-10 cents a word upon publication. Occasional feature: Short excerpts from novels in progress, by both published and unpublished writers.

Poetry: They are looking for poetry of all kinds—from sonnets to the prose poem. They pay $1.00 per line on publication. Poetry can be experimental, traditional, blank verse, free verse, etc. though no longer than 40 lines.

Reprints: Writer Online is currently accepting queries regarding reprints (previously published articles) in any of the above categories. They pay $20. for Second Serial (reprint) rights.

Content: Writers are advised to read current and archived Writer Online articles to obtain a sense of editorial values: http://www.novalearn.com/wol http://www.novalearn.com/wol/archivesTOC.htm

Send all unsolicited articles, fiction or poetry embedded in the body of an email, to creosote1@hotmail.com. Queries: Send email queries to creosote1@hotmail.com
    You may also send proposed articles, queries, and writing samples to:
Editor, Writer Online
40 Royal Oak Drive
Rochester, NY 14624
USA

3 A.M Publishing (L)
www.3ampublishing.com

3amPublishing is a mix of reviews, information, fiction, satire, popular journalism, e-books, and short stories. This is another website that is looking for contemporary material, with a fresh take. Anything entertaining and with an edge will make them sit up and take notice.

Category: Literary.
Frequency: Updated regularly.
Contact: editor@3ampublishing.com
Editor: Andrew Gallix.
Publisher: Kenneth Wilson.
Cost: Free.
Language: English.
Rights: They generally ask for first 90-day exclusive Internet rights with a one year option for archiving. First 90-day exclusive Internet rights means that they have the right for the first publishing of a story on the website for a 90-day run. The one-year option for archiving means that while the story is theirs exclusively for the first 90 days, the author is free to get it published elsewhere on the web even though it appears in archives for up to a year.
Payment: None.
Reply Time: This varies depending on workload and if they are in the progress of completing an issue. It could range anywhere from 1 week to 4 months. You might want to inquire about the current status of their "reading periods."

Guidelines and submission procedures:

They prefer stories to be between 3000 - 10,000 words in length, although if you have an exceptionally entertaining/intriguing piece, they will consider it. They are looking for on-edge and original (funky and fresh) fiction and non-fiction: comedy, action/adventure, satire, and horror. They are not looking for fan-fiction or stories that promote hate or racial bigotry.

Send completed short story/stories by email in plain text format to editor@3ampublishing.com. Please skip lines between paragraphs, and also place < p > tags at the beginning of each paragraph to ensure that formatting is not lost while in electronic transfer. Be sure to include information on how to contact you, i.e. a telephone number and email address. No snail mail submissions.

A few more ezines to consider, just as a final note:

Lit Kit

www.georgejr.com

This site includes interviews with authors and extracts from soon-to-be-published works, and essays on literature. Email George Myers Jr. with any ideas. They don't pay but the site is pretty slick. Email: editor@litkit.comNOSPAM.

Serpentinia

www.serpentinia.com

California based ezine. Runs an annual short story contest with prize money, and supports 'emerging' writers. Publishes poetry, prose, and short stories 'where the internal is universalised, the unconscious made conscious, and the unity of all opposites: man & woman; good & evil; creation & destruction; black & white; life & death; and body & spirit are acknowledged.' Whatever that means. No payment.

Email: publisher@serpentinia.com.

12Gauge

www.12gauge.com

Ezine based in Brooklyn, New York. Has moved from hard copy to publishing exclusively online. High quality publication. No payment.

Fiction: 4,000 words maximum. Poetry: No more than 5 poems per submission.

Essays, Reviews, Etc.: 1,000 words maximum. Artwork (photographs, line art, pen-and-ink sketches, paintings, comics, computer-generated art): Maximum of five pieces. Email: info@12gauge.com.

Linnaean St

www.linnaeanstreet.com

A strong literary focus. Features stories and novel excerpts, and essays. Email query before submitting material: wilsonbrosa@mediaone.net. No payment.

QUICK REFERENCE

Who wants what?

Afterimage
http://www.vsw.org/afterimage
Feature Articles/Reviews/Reports/Essays/News

Anotherealm
http://Anotherealm.com/
Fiction/Flash fiction

Back Brain Recluse
http://www.bbr-online.com/magazine
Fiction/Photos/Art

BackPacker Magazine
http://www.backpacker.com
Articles/Photography

Banking Strategies Magazine
http://www.bai.org/bankingstrategies
Feature Articles

Circle of Poets
http://www.taddgroup.com/poetry_newsletter.htm
Poetry

Computer Currents
http://www.currents.net
How-to/Technology overview/Consumer investigation/Buyers guide/Reviews

Comrades
http://www.safesurfer.co.uk/ezine/index2.htm
Short stories/Poetry /Artwork /Non-fiction & Memoirs

CyberAge Adventures
http://www.cyberageadventures.com/
Fiction/Art

Fiction Writer's Guideline
http://www.fictionwriters.com
How-to articles/Practical tips/Advice/Interviews/Success stories

History Today
www.historytoday.co.uk
Articles

Hope magazine
http://www.hopemag.com
Book Reviews/Essays/Photography and Illustration/Reports

I Love Cats Magazine
http://www.iluvcats.com
Fiction/Non fiction/No poetry/Articles/Photos/Drawings

Inkspot
www.inkspot.com
Short fiction/Poetry/Articles/Interviews

Inscriptions Magazine
http://www.inscriptionsmagazine.com
Articles/Interviews/Humour/Book Reviews

Insomnia zine
www.insomniazine.co.uk
Reviews/Photography/Comment/Editorial/Interviews/Artwork/profiles/Artic les/Contemporary fiction & non fiction/

Interchange
www.aber.ac.uk/~engwww/INTERCHANGE.htm
Poetry/Notes/Critical Essays

Intertext
www.intertext.com
Fiction/Humour/Essay/Non fiction articles

Jackhammer Ezine
http://www.eggplant-productions.com/jackhammer/
Speculative fiction

Kudzu
www.etext.org/kudzu
Poetry/Fiction/Essays

Let's Live Magazine
http://www.letsliveonline.com
Articles

littlemuch4women.com
http://www.littlemuch4women.com
Poetry/ Fiction or non-fiction/ Short stories/Articles/Book reviews/Writer's tips/Editor's Choice.

millenniumSHIFT webzine
http://www.millenniumshift.com
Prose/Poetry/Articles/Imagery/Story excerpts

New Tribal Dawn webzine

http://www.grailmedia.com/wz1/info/guidelines.html

Articles/Relevant news/Current events/Critical interviews/ Historical photographs/Brief news items/Letters to the editor.

New Woman Online

www.newwomanonline.co.uk

Features/Articles/News

Nocturne

http://www.impure.org/myrrh

Poetry/New writing/Fiction/Artwork/Writer's Forum/Critiques/Articles

Overland Express

www.overlandexpress.org/

New Poetry/Prose/Fiction

Pif Magazine

www.pifmagazine.com

Short fiction/Poetry/Essays/Reviews

Poetry.St Corner

http://www.Poetry.St/

Poetry/Prose/Verse

Quantum Muse

www.quantummuse.com

Artwork/Fiction/Serialisations

Quill

http://www.spj.org

Articles/Photo/Art

Richmond Review
http://www.richmondreview.co.uk
Short stories/Reviews/Articles

SageBase
http://www.sagebase.com
Non-fiction articles

Salon Magazine
www.salon.com
Articles

SilverKris
www.singaporeair.com
Travel & Adventure stories/Articles/

Slope
www.slope.org
Poetry/Reviews/Interviews

Spike
www.spikemagazine.com
Book Reviews/Interviews/Features/Articles

Stark Raving Sanity - An Electronic Literary Journal
http://www.StarkRavingSanity.com
Poetry/Short Stories/Theoretical works/Critical essays/Artwork

The Charlotte Austin Review - formerly The Quill
www.charlotteaustinreviewltd.com
Book Reviews/Interviews/Short fiction/Reflections/Features

The Edge
www.users.globalnet.co.uk/~houghtong/index.htm
Fiction/Features/Interviews/Novel Reviews/Comment columns

The Fiction Writer
www.fictionwriter.com
Articles/Tricks & tips/Interviews/Submission advice

The Mystery Review
www.inline-online.com/mystery/
Reviews/Interviews/Bookstore profiles/Word games/Puzzles/Photos/Art
Short filler articles/Illustrations:

The Rue Bella
www.ruebella.co.uk
Poetry/Short Stories

The Write Moves
http://www.allthewritemoves.com
Articles/How-to/Marketing/Research techniques, or anything else pertaining
to freelance web writing.

The Writer's Block Emagazine
http://writersblock808.homestead.com/guidelines.html
Non-fiction/ Fiction/ Short stories/Novel excerpts/Poetry/Horror/Science
Fiction/Fantasy/Romance/Personal experience essays.

Web del Sol
www.webdelsol.com
New media/Photography/Poetry/Fiction

Wild and Whirling Words
www.wildandwhirlingwords.com
Fiction

WorldJournalist.com
http://WorldJournalist.com
Articles

World Wide Freelance Writer
www.worldwidefreelance.com
Articles

Writers Online
http://www.novalearn/wol
Articles/Fiction/Poetry

3 A.M Publishing
www.3ampublishing.com
Popular Journalism/E-books/Short Stories

Who pays what?

Afterimage
http://www.vsw.org/afterimage
Payment: 0.5c/wd for articles, with a maximum of $100 for news, reports and reviews; $150 for essays; and $300 for features.

Anotherealm
http://Anotherealm.com/
Payment: US$10 per story, upon acceptance.

Back Brain Recluse
http://www.bbr-online.com/magazine
Payment: £10 ($15) per 1,000 words. Pays around $30 US for art/photos on publication per black and white full page used.

BackPacker Magazine
http://www.backpacker.com
Payment: $0.60 to $1.00 per word, depending upon the complexity and demands of the article, as well as the proven experience of the writer. Cover photos: $550-800. Photo use inside magazine: $100-400 (depends upon size and placement). Assignment day rate: $400-450

Banking Strategies Magazine
http://www.bai.org/bankingstrategies
Payment: $1.20/word for features to 2,500 words.

Computer Currents
http://www.currents.net
Payment: $1,500 to $2,000.

CyberAge Adventures
http://www.cyberageadventures.com/
Payment: They offer you a choice of compensation methods. They pay $0.02 to

$0.05 per word depending on your previous writing credits. Alternately, they offer you the chance to be a hero yourself by allowing them to make a donation in your name to the charity of your choice.

Fiction Writer's Guideline
http://www.fictionwriters.com
Payment: Range from $1 to $25, depending upon length and subject matter.

Hope magazine
http://www.hopemag.com
Payment: .50c/wd for text, and about $300 for a full-page editorial.

I Love Cats Magazine
http://www.iluvcats.com
Payment: $50-200 depending on the story for 500-1,500 words. Pays on publication. Artwork: Pays $25-250 for a cover. Short fillers: $25. Non-fiction: $50.

Inkspot
www.inkspot.com
Payment: 6c/wd, U.S. funds, on publication. If they choose to publish the article in both Inkspot and Inklings, pay is an additional 3c/wd.

Inscriptions Magazine
http://www.inscriptionsmagazine.com
Payment: Articles and Interviews: $40.00, or they will include a 50-word text ad (run within the ezine) or a banner ad (up to 7k) run on the Website for up to four weeks. Humour: $5 for each accepted and published humour items. Reviews: $5 for each accepted review.

Jackhammer Ezine
http://www.eggplant-productions.com/jackhammer/
Payment: An initial $25 (US)-upon return of signed and dated contract-and .50 (US) for each day the story is posted on the website after an initial one month period.

Let's Live Magazine
http://www.letsliveonline.com
Payment: $700 for departments, $800-1000 for features.

littlemuch4women.com
http://www.littlemuch4women.com
Payment: $5.00 per submission upon acceptance.

millenniumSHIFT webzine
http://www.millenniumshift.com
Payment: $10.00 US for each item published

New Tribal Dawn webzine http://www.grailmedia.com/wz1/info/guidelines.html
Payment: $50 per text article, upon acceptance.

Overland Express
www.overlandexpress.org/
Payment: Poems: A$70; Prose: $100; Hypertext: $100.

Pif Magazine
www.pifmagazine.com
Payment: Poetry (less than 100 lines) = $5 - $50 per poem. Short Stories (1,000 - 4,000 words) = $10-$50 per story. Micro Fiction (less than 500 words) = $5 - $50 per story. Commentary = $10-$50 per article. Review = $5-$50 per review

Quill
http://www.spj.org
Payment: From $100 for short pieces to $1,200 for major cover articles.

SageBase
http://www.sagebase.com
Payment: $20 after 3 months on site plus bonuses.

SilverKris

www.singaporeair.com

Payment: Basic rates are S$250 per 1,000 published words. Payment for photos depends on published size - S$200 for double-page spread or less, S$100 for full page or less, S$75 for half page or less, S$50 for quarter page or less, S$250 for cover. Photo essays are paid at a flat rate, regardless of the number of photos used - S$1,000 for four pages, S$1,250 for six pages and S$1,500 for eight pages.

The Edge

www.users.globalnet.co.uk/~houghtong/index.htm

Payment: Negotiable (up to £65 per 1000 words).

The Fiction Writer

www.fictionwriter.com

Payment: $50

The Write Moves

http://www.allthewritemoves.com

Payment: $10 upon acceptance.

The Writer's Block Emagazine

http://writersblock808.homestead.com/guidelines.html

Payment: $5 per piece upon publication.

WorldJournalist.com

http://WorldJournalist.com

Payment: you choose

World Wide Freelance Writer

www.worldwidefreelance.com

Payment: HK$160 (Hong Kong Dollars) (approx. US$20) per article.

Writers Online

http://www.novalearn.com/wol

Payment: Poetry $1.00 per line. Fiction/Non-fiction 5-10c per word. Reprints $20.00.

EZINES	WORD CONTENT	FLAT FEE	PAYMENT PER WORD	INCOME PROSPECTS
LITERARY				
INKSPOT	500-800 words shorter rather than longer		US$ 0.06 UK£ 0.04	US$ 39.00 UK£ 26.00 For 650 words
THE EDGE		(Edge buys all rights)	UK£ 0.65 US$ 0.975	UK£ 65.00 US$ 97.50 For 1000 words
PIF	Poetry 100 lines Micro fiction under 500 Commentary/review Short stories 1000 to 4000 words	All at US$ 5.00-50.00 UK£ 3.33-33.30 US $ 10.00-50.00 UK $ 6.66-33.30		Pif is regarded as the showcase
NON-FICTION				
AFTER IMAGE	Review 700-1500 Essays 1500-3000 Features 4000-6000		US$ 0.05 UK£ 0.033	Max. US$ 100-UK£ 66.66 Max. US$ 150-UK£ 100.00 Max. US$ 300-UK£ 200.00
BACKPACKER	1250-1750+		From US$ 0.60-UK£ 0.40 to US$ 1.00-UK£ 0.66 Depending on complexity	From US$ 900-UK£ 600 to US$ 1,500-UK£ 990 For 1,500 words

EZINES	WORD CONTENT	FLAT FEE	PAYMENT PER WORD	INCOME PROSPECTS
BANKING STRATEGIES	2500	(Banking buys all rights)	US$ 1.20 UK£ 0.80	US$ 3,000.00 UK£ 2,000.00 For 1,500 words
COMPUTER CURRENTS	Reviews 300-600 Stories 4000-10,000	US$ 1,500 to US$ 2,000 UK£ 1,000 to UK£ 1333 (Computer buys all rights)		US$ 1,500 to $ 2,000 UK£ 1,000 to £ 1,333
FICTION WRITERS	250-1200	US$ 25.00-UK£ 16.66		US$ 25.00-UK£ 16.66
HOPE	Features 1500-6000 Essays 1000-4000 Notes 200-600	Hope buys all rights	US$ 0.50 UK£ 0.33	US$ 300-UK£ 200 For full page editorial US$ 1,000-UK£ 666.66 For 2,000 words
CATS	500-1500	US$ 50.00-200.00 UK£ 33.00-133.00 Depending on story		US$ 50.00-UK£ 33.33 to US$ 200.00-UK£ 133.33
INSCRIPTIONS	articles 500-1500 humour under 1000 reviews 300-500	US$ 40.00-UK£ 26.00 US$ 5.00-UK£ 3.00		US$ 5.00 to $ 40.00 UK£ 3.3 to £ 26.66
LETS LIVE	Articles 1200-2000 Departments	US$ 700.00-UK£ 466.66 US$ 800.00 to $ 1,000.00		US$ 700.00 to $ 1,000.00 UK£ 466.66 to £ 666.66

EZINES	WORD CONTENT	FLAT FEE	PAYMENT PER WORD	INCOME PROSPECTS
	Features	UK£ 533.33 to £ 666.66 Lets live buys world 1st rights		
LITTLE MUCH WOMEN	Poetry/fiction Reviews/articles	US$ 5.00 UK£ 3.33		US$ 5.00 UK£ 3.33
MILLENNIUM SHIFT	800 or less varied categories	US$ 10.00 UK£ 6.66		US$ 10.00 UK£ 6.66
NEW TRIBAL DAWN	Articles 1500-3000 (Shorter acceptable)	US$ 50.00 UK£ 33.33		US$ 50.00 UK£ 33.33
OVERLANDS	Poems Prose Hypertext	AUS$ 70.00-UK£ 25.36 AUS$ 100.00-UK£ 36.23 AUS$ 100.00-UK£ 36.23		AUS$ 70.00 to $ 100.00 UK£ 25.36 to £ 36.23
QUILL	Short pieces Major articles	US$ 100.00-UK£ 66.66 US$ 1,200.00-UK£ 800.00 Quill buys 1st world rights		US$ 700.00 to $ 1,200.00 UK£ 66.66 to £ 800.00
SAGE BASE	200-1000	US$ 20.00 UK£ 13.33		US$ 20.00 UK£ 13.33
SILVERKRIS	per 1000 Travel/adventure/	SING$ 250.00 US$ 148.20		SING$ 250.00 US$ 148.20

EZINES	WORD CONTENT	FLAT FEE	PAYMENT PER WORD	INCOME PROSPECTS
	+ wide range	UK£ 98.80 (SK buys 1st Asian rights)		UK£ 98.80
THE INFORMER	1300-1800		US$ 0.08 UK£ 0.053	US$ 120.00 UK£ 79.50 For 1,500 words
WRITERS BLOCK	1500 max. Fiction/non-fiction	US$ 10.00 UK£ 6.66		US$ 10.00 UK£ 6.66
WRITE MOVES	800-1000 any aspect web weiting/publishing	US$ 10.00 UK£ 6.66 Write buys 1st electronic/archive rights		US$ 10.00 UK£ 6.66
WORLD WIDE FREELANCE	800-1000 for international freelance markets	Hongkong$ 160.00 US$ 22.00 UK£ 15.00 World Wide buys Website		Hongkong$ 160.00 US$ 22.00 UK£ 15.00
WORLD JOURNALIST	First electronic content market			You fix the price

EZINES	WORD CONTENT	FLAT FEE	PAYMENT PER WORD	INCOME PROSPECTS
GENRE EZINES				
ANOTHER REALM	Flash fiction 2000 Fiction 5000	US$ 10.00 UK£ 6.66		US$ 10.00 UK£ 6.66
BACK BRAIN RECLUSE	Science fiction	Back Brain buys first English language rights	US$ 15.00 UK£ 10.00 Per 1,000 words	US$ 15.00 UK£ 10.00 Per 1,000 words
CYBERAGE ADVENTURES	Short short fiction 1500 Short fiction 3000		US$ 0.02 to $ 0.05 UK£ 0.013 to £ 0.033	US$ 30.00-UK£ 19.50 For 1500 words US$ 150.00-UK£ 100 For 3,000 words
JACKHAMMER	Notes/essays 1500 Fiction 3000	US$ 25.00 UK£ 16.66		US$ 0.50-UK£ 0.33 Per day for every day posted after first month

Exchange Rates: £1 UK =

US$ 1.50
Singapore$ 2.53
HongKong$ 10.81
Australian$ 2.76

2

E-BOOK PUBLISHING

What is an e-book?

An e-book is simply a book. The difference lies in the construction; rather than going though the print process, an electronic book is formatted to fit on your computer screen, e-book reader or a device like a Palm Pilot, in a variety of programmes.

E-books can be printed out or read on your computer, reader or laptop screen or they can be stored on diskettes, CD-ROMS or downloaded and viewed on your computer screen, on a PDA, or on an electronic reading device like a Rocket eBook. Simply put, e-books are books presented in a digital format instead of traditional ink and paper. The new reading platforms, called e-book readers, are small, lightweight, battery-operated, rechargeable devices that have enough memory to store several e-books at one time. PDA's were the forerunners of the technology behind the latest e-book readers, first pioneered by Apple Computer which introduced the Newton MessagePad in 1993. Short for 'personal digital assistant', these are handheld devices that combine computing, telephone/fax, and networking features. A typical PDA can function as a cellular phone, fax sender, and personal organiser. Unlike portable computers, most PDA's use a stylus (pen) rather than a keyboard for input.

Print and electronic publishing are not dissimilar. An author still has to write, edit and submit a book in whatever format; the book is then either accepted or rejected by the publisher or e-publisher. The real difference lies in the final product: a tangible product like a book that you can hold in your hand or an electronic version. The fact still remains that the final product in both cases can be good or bad. Most e-publishers have been so inundated with manuscripts they have to close submissions for a period of time. They can afford to be selective with more than ninety percent of submissions ultimately being rejected.

There are close to four million PDA's in use, notably COM's Palm Pilot and so it would be reasonable to project that this could rise to at least ten million in 2001. The software to display large text files is available in all PDA's, and a steadily increasing numbers of PDA owners now use these devices to read documents and books.

How do I read an e-book?

E-books can be printed out and read like a traditional book or read on the screen of a desktop or laptop computer, a PDA or a dedicated e-book reader. There are special formats for reading e-books on your computer, e-book readers and PDA's. This format makes many e-books available to people who do not own an e-book reader.

The Microsoft Reader
www.microsoft.com/reader.

The Microsoft Reader is an e-book reading program available for PC's (the software is available for free download from the site) and the Pocket PC (which comes with the software already installed and 30 titles, although you can get more from Barnes & Noble). Page layout on the PC resembles that of a paper book. ClearType™ display technology brings the look and feel of high-resolution printing to on-screen reading. You can highlight, bookmark, make notes, look up definitions and save easily. You can change the font size and use the backlight to read in the dark. All the books and other content that you acquire are stored in the Microsoft Reader Library. The Microsoft reader also enables you to create large print editions of any book from the Quick Settings page. The PocketPC is a lightweight hand held reader, which also uses ClearType™ display, and a book-like user interface that eliminates icons and buttons. Microsoft Reader is available on Pocket PC devices manufactured by Hewlett-Packard, Casio, and Compaq.

Adobe Acrobat

www.acrobat.com,

Adobe Acrobat offers another book reading programme. It creates files that can be displayed on most platforms, and most e-publishers offer books for download in PDF because it is so versatile. It is easy to use, has a small file size and the page layout is unsurpassed. It is already an e-book industry standard. It does have a new font, Clear Type, which has been designed specifically for screen usage. A computer screen consists of thousands of small dots, pixels, which compose the picture. Clear Type can make each pixel display more than one colour, so they are less 'blocky', and the smoother image is easier to read. Both the Microsoft eReader and Adobe Acrobat systems enable the user to access e-books through their PDA's. Adobe is also coming out with a secure upgrade for Acrobat that will make e-books almost 100% safe against the e-book black-market.

Glassbook Reader

www.glassbook.com

The Glassbook reader is a free software program for reading electronic books on your laptop or desktop PC and is available for free download from the site. It provides a full-color display of e-book pages including, Adobe PDF documents, and a two page display for reading. You can highlight text and annotate e-book passages. The Glassbook Plus Reader offers the same technology as the reader but supports industry standards that guarantee access to a wide variety of e-books. The Glassbook Plus Reader displays e-books in Adobe Portable Document Format (PDF), and also displays e-books that use the new Open eBook Publication Structure (OEB) format.

Rocket eBook/Gemstar eBook

(Rocket-eBook.com and SoftBook.com are now eBook-Gemstar.com)

www.ebook-gemstar.com

Rocket eBooks are about the size and weight of a traditional book. The professional edition of the Rocket weighs about a pound and a half, has an adjustable backlight, and can store about four million words of text, or about forty novels. Using the stylus included with the Rocket, you can highlight text and then underline it, bring up its definition, and set a bookmark. You can use the search feature to find specific text, and jump around from any place in your book to any other almost instantly. You can also switch the size of the reading font. The next generation Rocket eBook, the REB1100 ($300) and the REB1200 ($600) are on sale now with 10,000 titles available. Go to www.rca.com for a list of retailers. The REB 1100 is smaller, lighter and less expensive than the REB 1200. The REB 1200 features a color display that is more appropriate for magazines and both a 56K modem and an Ethernet port for fast book downloads. The REB 1100 can purchase books directly from an eBook catalogue throughout the internal 33.6K modem, or use the computer to download books from booksellers like Barnes and Noble or Powells, then transfer the digital content to the eBook through the infrared or USB port. The REB 1100 uses a Smart Media card for memory expansion, while the 1200 uses Compact Flash cards. Publishing Partners

The Rocket eBook is much more than just a reader or a site used for downloading e-books. They offer 45% royalties on books sold through them and a sole rights distribution network. You can also become a Rocket eBook publisher, but you must purchase one of the readers. The reader comes with a CD-ROM enabling you to transfer the Rocket eBook files from your PC to the reader. It also contains a conversion programme that will let you create your own Rocket eBooks. To display books on the Rocket site it is necessary to become a publisher. Five or more titles can be made available through a Distribution Agreement between the publisher and NuvoMedia. NuvoMedia will then distribute the RocketEdition of the work. The Publisher sets the price, and assigns an ISBN for the RocketEdition of each work. They sell the book to NuvoMedia at 55% discount who are then free to distribute that edition wherever they wish. You can visit the Rocket Library at www.rocket-library.com to submit and download e-books. They mostly deal with established publishers though.

However, in recent months there has been a veritable onslaught of new devices coming onto the market and announcements of those in development from established and new technology companies.

EBookMan

www.franklin.com/ebookman

Franklin Electronic Publishers have developed the eBookMan, a "multimedia reader and content player" that looks a lot like a PDA (and comes with PDA-type calendar and address book functions) but is much better suited to reading e-books than Palm-pilot type devices. The grey-scale screen is 200 pixels wide and 240 pixels high, displaying 87% more information than the Palm screen, enough for about 20 lines of text, depending on the font size. Franklin originally announced that the eBookMan would display Microsoft Reader titles but initially the units will be released on to the market with Franklin's own secure eBook reading software.

Korea eBook

www.hiebook.com

The new Korea eBook device has also been developed. It is quite lightweight and easy to hold, its size being somewhere between a PDA and the Rocket eBook. It has a black-and-white LCD touch screen with a full 480 x 320 pixels screen, the same as the Rocket eBook. The case has big buttons for paging forward and backward. Korea eBook Inc., the manufacturer, has already marketed a PC-based Korean-language eBook reading program called the Hiebook Reader (www.hiebook.com) as well as a tool for converting XML content for the Reader. The Korea eBook device will also play MP3 music files and perform standard PDA functions, including synchronisation with Outlook Express.

The Cybook

www.cytale.com

The Cybook from the French firm Cytale was the first to make its debut in Europe. The device, which is manufactured by Hitachi, has an anodised aluminium frame, a form factor, and a color LCD screen measuring 10 inches diagonally. The company's proprietary rendering software preserves the layout of a graphically complex page no matter which font size is selected. 40% of French publishers have signed up with Cytale to provide content for the devices, which use a format compatible with the Open eBook (OEB) standard. It costs in the region of £522.00.

GoReader
www.goreader.com

GoReader, a Chicago company of the same name has developed a prototype device called the goReader. The goReader has a color LCD touch screen that's 7.3 inches wide and 9.7 inches high, in a grey plastic case measuring 9.5 inches by 12.6 inches by about 1 inch thick. The prototype is heavy for an eBook reader, weighing almost 5lbs, but its has lots of features for making your own onscreen notes and highlights in multiple colours. The OEB-compliant device is aimed at university students, who will obtain textbook content directly from the goReader Web site.

It is predicted that by the year 2003 e-book readers will weigh less than one pound and cost in the region of £66.00 or $99.00. Sales of e-books, e-magazines and e-newspapers should reach £670m by 2005. Some commentators have predicted that 500,000 e-books will be available on the internet by the end of the year and Worldwide sales of e-books could hit £2.3bn in five years. There is still uncertainty over how the market will develop and many publishers and technology providers are proceeding cautiously. The UK is currently playing catch-up; Rocket eBooks are not on the market in the UK, although we are promised the Rocket eBook within a year. But Microsoft is offering a free download of its reader software to all Microsoft Windows 95 (or later) operating systems on desktop and laptop computers. Visit http://www.microsoft.com/reader/ for more details.

The Open eBook Forum

The Open eBook initiative was announced at the world's first electronic book conference in October 1998. The Open eBook Authoring Group was formed to address the problem of file formats for e-books. In September 1999, the Group released Version 1.0 of the new file specification (the Open eBook Publication Structure 1.0) for e-book publication.

Software companies are currently working to produce applications that will convert existing file formats (Adobe PDF, MS Word, WordPerfect) into the new specification. This will ensure that readers will not be faced with competing technologies, and means that everyone will be able to buy e-books and know that they will work on all media.

The OeBF has launched a standards co-ordination initiative to bring together developments in e-book and e-publishing platforms. Simply put, they are trying to create a level playing field in the industry, and within this they are also tackling areas like digital rights management (DRM). Details can be found at http://www.openebook.org/framework. The framework intends to provide initiatives and solutions that will meet the needs of authors, publishers, libraries and other investors in the e-book market. They are looking to create a 'common vocabulary' and use this to work towards digital rights management that will ease the movement of e-books to readers and create a standard in the industry that will ensure everyone is talking the same language. The OeBF is simply helping to define those standards and ensure that the electronic book becomes available, accessible and at a reasonable price.

Why e-publish?

The e-publishing industry is taking off and although many print based publishers are being cautious in their approach to it, many smaller e-publishers already on the internet are convinced that e-books are the future. They see themselves filling the chasm left by the demise of the small publisher. Most only accept work of the highest quality and all are trying to provide readers with a broader choice than they currently have. If you are still in any doubt about the benefits of e-publishing, read on:

- The production and distribution costs are considerably less than for traditional printed books.
- This makes e-books generally much cheaper both to produce and to buy.
- E-book publishers can take a chance on books the big publishing houses can't or won't publish.

- E- books don't need either shelves or bookstores. Since e-books can be downloaded, readers can begin enjoying their new books within minutes after purchase.
- E-books are paperless publishing and so save trees.
- E-publishing can be a more welcoming environment for the first time author. In reality it is very hard to get published by a print publisher unless you have an agent and a proven sales record, particularly in the US.
- E-publishing as an industry has exploded over the last year. E-book reading has taken off and with the advent of specialist handheld devices and advances in technology making the price of this technology cheaper the market will become more accessible to everyone.
- The royalties are higher, some e-book publishers offering 50% and upwards.
- The time it takes to produce an e-book is much shorter than a traditional print version, which means your material will be available sooner.
- The internet provides a global market for your work.

Having said this, it is important to select an e-publisher with care. Some e-publishers on the internet are no more than cyber vanity publishers, publishing anything that is sent to them and offering no editorial control. Be particularly careful of sites that require payment for services. However, most have rigorous editorial processes and do not ask for payment to publish your work. You must consider what you are expecting from your e-publisher in order to select the one that suits your needs. It always helps to make a detailed study of the available market. Compare and contrast individual e-publishers and you will then be able to make an informed choice based on the knowledge you have gained. Use the checklist below to start with; if the answers to the questions, and any others you can think of, are not fully dealt with on the website then do query the editor or publisher of the site. There are a number of websites that provide resources for writers who have already published electronically or are thinking about it, try:

eBooks N'Bytes

www.ebooksnbytes.com

They specialise in resources for e-book publishers, and publish a regular email newsletter, which includes e-book related tips, news and reviews.

eBook Connections

www.ebookconnections.com

Comprehensive guide to everything 'e-book' related, including primers on how to read an e-book and why to e-publish.

eBookNet.com

www.ebook.net

Good resource for author's considering e-publishing, including up to date news on the industry and information about writing and reading e-books.

E-books.org

www.E-books.org

This web site provides a repository of information related to e-book research and products, focusing primarily on document readers, their possibilities and limitations.

Bibliofuture

www.bibliofuture.homepage.com

Bibliofuture is attempting to be a resource where librarians can find out about the changes that are happening because of e-book readers.

Which e-publisher?

The e-book publishers featured in the handbook are just the tip of the iceberg; new ones are appearing on a daily basis. Possibly you will recognise some of the names, such as Online Originals and Hard Shell Word Factory; these companies have been operating for a number of years, others may not be so familiar. They come in all shapes and sizes, and those that are listed should provide you with a good chance to compare and contrast different approaches and services.

The e-publishers listed have been chosen for a variety of reasons:

- They publish a particular genre.
- They are well placed in the e-publishing industry.
- They offer a good choice of services to writers.
- Their editorial standards are particularly high.

Selecting an e-publisher is not easy and there are a number of factors to take into consideration. Although the details provided in this handbook are fairly comprehensive the onus still rests with the writer, and that means you, as the writer, must do effective research to find the one that suits you the best. If you are thinking of e-publishing then try actually buying an e-book. Experience the process first hand. All of us have bought print books, browsed through a bookshop and made a purchase, taken the book home, sat back in a comfy chair and begun reading. We all have our favourite bookshop because we like the way it is set out and like the ambience, the helpful staff; we are all familiar with the process. But if you haven't been through the process of buying an e-book, how can you possibly judge what e-publishing is all about? Is the process painless or difficult, did the download take a long time, was the credit card transaction simple, what does it feel like to read an e-book from a screen? Until you know the answers to all these questions, how can you select an e-publisher? The answer is, you can't. And if you, as the writer, aren't prepared to buy an e-book then why should anyone else?

A checklist for choosing the right e-publishing site:

- Does the site have an 'about us' page that provides information about the business and the people who run it. A good company will give details of how long they have been operating, the names of staff members and contact details, a business address and phone number. Look to see if they are affiliated to any associations or trade or publishers' groups.
- Is the e-publisher charging for their services and if so, how much?

- Look at the authors' pages. If they list email addresses you could email an author and ask them a few questions about the site.
- Do they cover the genre you are interested in publishing?
- Are their guidelines detailed enough?
- Do they edit manuscripts or are manuscripts published on an 'as is' basis? This is an important question, since editing is the key to the production of quality material.
- What publishing formats are available?
- Does the site provide a sample contract?
- Are royalties payable to you and if so, what percentage?
- Does the site have an effective marketing campaign?
- Can you display your work elsewhere or does the contract restrict the use of your material?
- Are the sales and e-commerce facilities on the site good?
- Do they issue ISBN's?
- How will your e-book be promoted?
- When will your royalties be paid, e.g. six-monthly, quarterly?

There are disadvantages to e-publishing but most of the arguments against it come from traditionally published authors who argue that those published solely on the internet are not 'real authors'. They go so far as to restrict them from joining their organisations or entering their competitions and awards. But surely the only criteria should be the quality of the work; the format is secondary.

E-publishing is a technology that is prone to rapid change and the ramifications of it are reverberating throughout the publishing industry at the moment and will continue to do so into the future. It will take some time for things to settle down but in the meantime authors such as Stephen King and Frederick Forsyth have plunged into the e-publishing world with an enthusiasm that is heart warming. At least they are prepared to give it a try, rather than rejecting it out of hand. E-books have gained ground in the past year and will continue to forge ahead, bringing new readers and writers who are prepared to champion the cause. Any reluctance on the part of traditional writers will not hold back the tide of new voices, who view e-publishing as an additional market for their work rather than competition and who will wish their work to stand on its own merits.

The life of an 'e-author' is no different to that of many mainstream authors; they have agents, promotional conferences, appear as guests on the radio, television and chat rooms, are interviewed for articles and are also invited to speak to writers' groups. The traditionally published author seems hungry for information about e-publishing. Many authors are published both traditionally and electronically and believe there is very little difference in the final product. The lines are continually being crossed and the point is that 'e-authors' are not authors who couldn't get published any other way. The book in its traditional form is not dead; it has just been given a new lease of life.

Submitting your manuscript

It's simple; read the guidelines and submission procedures and follow them. If you are in any doubt email a query before you submit; the quickest way to get a rejection is to ignore the guidelines and hope they won't notice - they will. If they don't publish science fiction, don't send them science fiction; if they ask for the manuscript embedded in an email, don't send it as a file attachment. Make sure your manuscript is presented well; edit and proofread it before you send it to them. If you are unsure of any submission terms please refer to the ezine section of the handbook where many of these are explained in detail.

Many e-publishers will respond fairly quickly to submissions but as the industry takes off you may find response time getting slower. If you haven't heard anything within three months, then simply send a polite email requesting information on the status of your submission.

E-book Publishers
[An a-z listing]

AGoodBook.com
www.agoodbook.com

They feature a handful of published books, which they refer to as their Gutenberg books/treeware, and a few new titles, which they refer to as Cyberbooks/e-books. Their book list is short and some of their published books are available to buy through Amazon. They offer a free monthly newsletter which includes opinions and new book information. They charge a fairly hefty reading fee and compared to other e-publishers their royalties are pretty low. Downloadable formats are restricted to PDF and although they ask for quality they might have to offer better payments to authors if they are expecting to achieve this.

Category: Romance, comedy, adventure, literature and self-help.
Contact: editor@agoodbook.com.
Editor: Steven Bassion.
Royalties: 20% of the selling price for all copies sold, less a reserve for credit card disputes. Initially, this reserve will be 10% of royalties and will be adjusted up or down based on actual, documented experience. Accounting for royalties will be made monthly, on the 25th of each month, for the preceding month.
Rights: A purchase will be in the form of the right to download the book in digital form through the internet.
Fees: $250 reading fee.
Contract: The work will be offered for sale for a period of one year from notice of acceptance .
Formats: Adobe PDF.
Editorial Control: The submitted work will be read thoroughly and reviewed.
Acceptance policy: No guarantee of publication is made by acceptance of the appraisal fee.
ISBN: None.
Average book price: $4.95.

Additional Services: None.

Reply Time: Current book review time is approximately 6 weeks from the date AgoodBook receives the manuscript and payment of the reading fee.

Submissions guidelines and procedures:

1. Read and accept the Author's Agreement, you must pre-pay the $250 reading fee when you accept the agreement. You may pay by credit card using their secured payment system or you may mail a cheque or money order.

2. You must submit the book via email, after receiving a registration number from AGoodBook. Keep copies. The file should be saved in a "Text Only" or "ASCII" format prior to emailing. If you choose, you may file a copyright application with the Library of Congress to protect yourself. If you have any questions email the editor.

3. When you email the manuscript, include a letter stating your name and address and agreement number. State in the letter how you prefer to be contacted - by letter, fax or email.

4. Prospective authors may expect to receive a response within 6 weeks of receipt of manuscript and reading fee.

Allendale Online Publishing
www.allandale.co.uk

Allandale Online specialises in academic ebooks. They rely on an emerging network of ebooksellers to distribute their titles. At the moment its list is confined to Politics and International Relations but it expects to move into other areas. AOP is based in Leicester. It is managed by Simon Kear who employs for commissioning and editing a team of experienced academics. This is headed by G. R. Berridge, who is Professor of International Politics at the University of Leicester, general editor of a book series with a major London publishing house, and an associate editor on OUP's New Dictionary of National Biography.

Category: Academic.
Contact: md@allandale.co.uk
Editor: G.R. Berridge.
Royalties: 1.A flat rate of 30% of the net receipts on every ebook sold. 2.A flat rate of 30% of the net receipts after 100 ebooks have been sold.
Rights: An electronic rights-only contract, leaving authors free to seek printed book publication elsewhere (except where alternative terms have been mutually agreed).
Fees: None.
Contract: A fixed term licence of only five years, after which the author's rights will revert on request (see box on Reverted Rights), though they would like first refusal on any new contract.
Formats: Glassbook/MS Reader/Rocket eBook/The Glassbook/PDF Ebook
Editorial Control: Personal attention from one editor, from initial contact through to (and including) copy editing
Acceptance policy: AOP maintains rigorous editorial standards and reserves the right to decline manuscripts that are considered to be sub-standard.
ISBN: Each book has an ISBN, with its 'proper book' connotation and publicity advantages.
Average book price: £2.99.
Additional Services: None.
Reply Time: An opinion on a proposal within 4 weeks.

E-BOOK PUBLISHING

Submission guidelines and procedures:

AOP welcomes at the moment proposals (including mss.) for books or shorter works in the areas of Politics, International Relations, and International History, though it may move into other areas if the editorial expertise is available. They would prefer initial approaches from authors to take the form of a short synopsis or a message spelling out an idea. However, manuscripts will be accepted provided they contain a contents list and genuine preface. In either event, please also supply a curriculum vitae.

Authors should submit one hard copy of their proposal to the following address:

The Managing Director
Allandale Online Publishing
2 Park House
21 St Leonards Rd
Leicester LE2 1WS

Receipt of your proposal will be acknowledged. If accepted for publication, you will be made a formal offer of terms and, if these are accepted, you will be sent a draft contract very quickly. Your editor will remain with you through all stages up to production.

1. Proposals and manuscripts should not be under consideration for publication elsewhere.

2. Manuscripts must be submitted in MS Word format. If an index is included, this must be generated using Word's Index facility.

Tel/Fax: +44 -(0)116-210-0823

ArtemisPress
www.artemispress.com

ArtemisPress was launched in September of 2000 with a focus on the electronic publication and promotion of fiction and non-fiction works of interest to the international lesbian community. At the time the handbook was written the site was still under construction, although most of the pages were up and running. The site is good looking, easy to navigate and although no titles were available it seems prospects for the future are promising.

Category: Fiction/Non-fiction.
Contact: editor@artemispress.com.
Editor: Susan R Skolnick.
Royalties: 40% of the U.S. retail download price. 40% on outside sales made through online distributors, bookstores and other organisations.
Rights: First Rights of all electronic and digital versions.
Fees: None.
Contract:. Author or the publisher may terminate this contract with a 90-day written, certified mail notice.
Formats: HTML/PDF /Palm/Rocket eBook.
Editorial Control: Not stated.
Acceptance policy: Not listed.
ISBN: They will obtain an ISBN for your work, and will use the ISBN as part of the formal identification of that work.
Average book price:
Additional Services: None.
Reply Time: ASAP.

Submissions guidelines and procedures:

Manuscripts should be saved in MS Word (DOC) or Rich Text (RTF) format and named in the following manner: yourname_date.doc or yourname_date.rtf (where "yourname" represents your initials and last name.) A properly named file would look like this: mrjohnson_090100.doc. Your DOC or RTF file must be sent as an email attachment - do not send the manuscript in the body of your email message. The body of the email should contain only the following information: your name, pen name (if applicable), phone number, email address, manuscript title, genre/subgenre or subject category, file name and format (DOC or RTF) and the word processing program/version number used to create your manuscript.

Manuscripts should be formatted as follows:

–Do not use "macros" of any kind when saving your manuscript.

–Use Times Roman (or a similar serif font) in 12 pt size.

–Do not use special symbols or characters.

–Use single spacing, with a double space between paragraphs.

–Margins should be ragged right. (Do not justify the margins.)

–Use word wrap. (Do not use hard returns at the end of each line.)

–Paragraphs should be indented using tabs, not the spacebar.

–Use regular quotation marks, not "smart quotes" (curly quotes.)

–Use double dashes instead of em dashes.

–Use only one space at the end of a sentence, not two.

–Use italics in place of underlines.

–Do not use footers and headers.

–Place non-fiction citations, footnotes and references at the end of chapters.

–Do not use page numbers. Page numbers are irrelevant in electronic books.

–Chapter names/numbers should be in bold type.

–End the manuscript with the words "end" or "the end."

ArtemisPress.com
SRS Internet Publishing
236 West Portal Avenue, #525
San Francisco, California 94127
USA

Authors Online
www.authorsonline.co.uk

Authors Online is based in the UK, they charge quite a modest fee for services to previously published authors and additional hosting, but there is no editorial control in terms of quality; leaving this for readers to judge, which means they will publish any manuscript sent to them. They charge nothing to publish e-books. They maintain a fairly constant number of hits to the site, in the region of about 500 a day, and boast regular contact with traditional publishing houses. They offer a number of services to publishers who want to link to their site, including e-commerce and encryption and will pay 60% of the net revenue received by them.

Category: General Fiction and Non-fiction
Contact: theeditor@authorsonline.co.uk.
Editor: Richard Fitt.
Royalties: 60% net of the retail price, paid monthly.
Rights: Authors retain copyright and can negotiate with traditional publishers.
Fees: There is a one-off set up fee of £31.70 +VAT per text book for previously published authors. Followed by an annual "hosting" fee of £10 + VAT per text book which is due at the time of joining. Total cost including VAT £49.00.
Contract: When you find the right publisher your work can be removed from the site if required.
Formats: PalmPilot/E-Book reader
Editorial Control: They will read your book only to verify that it does not infringe any relevant law, and they reserve the right to refuse publication if necessary. Author retains editorial control at all times, and work can be removed from the site if required.
Acceptance policy: Not specifically stated.
ISBN: None.
Average book price: Prices vary from .95p to £2.95 + 50p credit card transaction fee.
Additional Services: You can submit further edited versions, which they will upload for a £10 administration cost. For a small administration cost they will supply you with the statistics (i.e. hits) on your page.
Reply Time: Immediate.

E-BOOK PUBLISHING

Submissions guidelines and procedures:

To place a book for sale on this site:

a) Send your "text only" work in electronic format (don't forget to copyright © it), in Microsoft Word PC/Mac format diskette.*

b) A synopsis of the story of not more than 200 words.

c) A note of which sample chapter the reader can browse, thus obtaining a flavour of your style.

d) A brief CV of yourself would also be useful, helping to sell your work.

e) Tell them which category to list your work under.

f) A description of your work in no more than 20-25 words.

g) Your costs cheque.

*If you are unable to send them a diskette they can offer you the following services:-

1) They will type from your manuscript or paper/hardback copy onto disk.

2) They will scan from your paper/hardback copy onto disk, however they will have to guillotine the spine. They can rebind if required.

Both 1) and 2) are chargeable, estimate £100-£200 depending on size.

1a Adams Yard,
HERTFORD
Herts
SG14 3DH
Telephone: 0044 1992 503151
Fax: 0044 1992 535424

avid press LLC
www.avidpress.com

Two sisters, Colleen Gleason Schulte and Kate Gleason founded avid Press. They both have backgrounds in editing and writing. They offer both electronic and print versions of books. The site is well planned, attractive and looks professional, because it works well and is easy to navigate whether you are a reader or an author. Their royalties are fairly low for the industry, but they offer print versions for no extra cost to the author.

Category: Fiction/Non-fiction.

Contact: Information: cgs@avidpress.com. Submissions: subs@avidpress.com.

Editor: Colleen Gleason Schulte and Kate Gleason.

Royalties: 30% in US$ of the retail download price. 10% of net received on print versions.

Rights: Exclusive world-wide rights to produce, publish, and sell in electronic format (including electronic download, disk, CD, or any other digital format known or to be invented). Any additional rights granted by the optional Print Format Addendum.

Fees: None.

Contract: Contract shall expire twelve (12) months from date of initial publication of electronic format.

Formats: HTML/RTF/PDF

Editorial Control: They will edit and revise work under the terms of the contract.

Acceptance policy: Not stated.

ISBN: They obtain ISBNs for authors.

Average book price: Download - $4.00. Diskette- $5.00. Print - $10.95.

Additional Services: Print versions.

Reply Time: 3-4 months.

Submissions guidelines and procedures:

Submissions should consist of the following information:
*   short synopsis in the body of the email

E-BOOK PUBLISHING

- general author bio
- first chapter or prologue only, as email attachment

Submissions will be accepted by email attachment in the following formats:
Word for Windows, version 6 or earlier
WordPerfect, version 8 or earlier
RTF format

Submissions will only be accepted at the following email address:
subs@avidpress.com

Snail mail submissions may be sent to:
Avid Press, LLC
5470 Red Fox Drive
Brighton, MI 48114-9079

Awe-Struck E-books
www.awe-struck.net

Awe-Struck E-Books offer titles in romance, sci-fi, sci-fi romance, non-fiction, and they have sign language software as well. Their e-books are also available at Barnes and Noble, Powells, and Peanut Press. Awestruck sends out widely distributed press releases.

Category: Fiction, including sci-fi and sci-fi romance/Non-Fiction.
Contact: kdstruck@home.com.
Editor: Dick Claassen, Kathryn D. Struck.
Royalties: 40%, paid quarterly.
Rights: Electronic rights. You are free to pursue agents and print publishers.
Contract: Two-year renewable contract.
Formats: Rocket eBook/Palm Pilot.
Editorial Control: They may ask you to make some changes to the content of your manuscript.
Acceptance policy: They are looking for high quality fiction.
ISBN: None.
Average book price: $4.30.
Additional Services: Extra files: $3.50 per file. Should the author decide to have his/her book distributed by NuvoMedia, there is a formatting fee of $50.00, payable in advance.
Reply Time: Three weeks to update you on its status in the reading queue or to ask for the complete manuscript and other necessary information.

Submissions guidelines and procedures:

Email a cover letter. Attach to the email a document including a short synopsis (2-4 pages is preferred), and the first two chapters only. Limit your email message to the cover letter. Do not include your synopsis and chapters in the email message. Do not send the entire manuscript unless they ask for it. The file you attach must be in Microsoft Word RTF format. You may also send a straight Microsoft Word file. The file you attach must be labelled with your last name. If you are sending a Win 3.1 file, label the file with the first 8 letters of your last name. If possible, compress the file before you attach it to your email.

Bookbooters

www.bookbooters.com

Bookbooters offers a high level of service. They are extremely selective, and maintain a strict editorial policy. All books published on the site will have been approved, proofread and edited by their staff. They require that you become a member but this is free and entitles you to access a number of resources. They list themselves as an e-book portal. To submit material to them you must become a member. Their book productions services are very competitive compared to similar services offered by other e-book publishers.

Category: All genres, including electronic adaptations of both original and classic works.
Contact: editor@bookbooters.com or submissions@bookbooters.com
Editor: Toby Emden.
Royalties: In addition to the 25%-50% you earn on all e-book sales of your novel, you will earn 25% on the net profits of paperback sales. Cheques will be mailed to the author no later than the third working day of each calendar month.
Rights: Authors retain exclusive copyright over their work and are free to do with it as they wish.
Fees: None
Contract: Authors can nullify the agreement at any time by giving 7 days' notice in writing, by email or fax.
Formats: Microsoft Word/Adobe Acrobat (PDF)/Rocket Book (RB)/HTML. They are also planning to release e-books in SoftBook and Pocket PC (Microsoft Reader) formats in the near future, and will consider any other e-book format as and when they become available.
Editorial Control: Once your novel has been accepted for e-publication, it will undergo proofreading and editing. Depending on the length of the novel, this may take several weeks.
Acceptance policy: If your manuscript is declined, they will always offer a detailed, constructive explanation of their reasons. In most cases, they will invite you to resubmit your manuscript once you have made any necessary modifications.
ISBN: ISBNs are assigned for print books.

Average book price: $4.00 and $15.00.

Additional Services: E-book production is free. They do however offer additional publishing services in the form of Silver and Gold membership. The Silver membership, if accepted, entitles you to have your book published in e-book format which you can then upgrade to Gold membership to have your book published in print form for a fee of $65.00. Following approval of your manuscript you will be able to complete the production process online. Once you have done this, they will mail you a hard copy of the General Authors' Publishing Agreement.

Reply Time: It will take approximately four to six weeks for them to review your novel. If they decide to proceed with publication, proofing and editing will take another two weeks.

Submissions guidelines and procedures:

To make a submission, you are required to be a Bookbooters Member. Lifetime membership of the Bookbooters Writers' Club is free and entitles you to various member benefits, such as access to a variety of articles by other members, a chat area and, in the near future, the option to have your novel published in bound copy for free.

Once a member, you can submit your novel for review. Simply follow the on-screen instructions on the site.

They accept submissions in Microsoft Word, Adobe Acrobat, Plain Text and Rich Text formats. Novels should be a minimum of 45,000 words in length. If using DOC or RTF format, paragraphs should be justified with a leading indent (tab) at the beginning of each paragraph. If using DOC or RTF format, standard font format should be Times New Roman, 12 Point, no bold. There are no restrictions on using other fonts for special text. Underlining should never be used in narrative unless absolutely necessary. If possible, try to use italics instead.

Bookbooters.com Inc.,
6 Alan Drive,
Weatogue, CT 06089

BiblioBytes
www.bibliobytes.com

BiblioBytes was founded in January 1993 by Glenn Hauman, Todd Masco, and Andrew Bressen. They made their first sales in July 1994 so they are one of the early front runners in e-publishing. All their books are available for free download. They are particularly keen to promote banned books and a large part of the site is dedicated to showcasing these books and discussing internet censorship.

Category: Fiction/Non-fiction
Contact: submission@bb.com
Editor: Glenn Hauman, Todd Masco, and Andrew Bressen (co-founders).
Royalties: BiblioBytes pays a royalty on revenues realized from sales of 35%, which may be amended from time to time by mutual agreement. Royalty statements are computed quarterly on March 31, June 30, September 30, and December 31 of each year.
Rights: Exclusive Internet rights.
Fees: None.
Contract: Contracts last for a period of five years unless terminated by either party upon sixty days' written notice.
Formats: MS Word/Word Perfect/WordStar/RTF. ASCII & HTML accepted under certain circumstances. You can email them if you have a different format.
Editorial Control: None, the manuscript will be published 'as is'.
Acceptance policy: If you follow their submission guidelines, you will most likely be accepted for publication.
ISBN: None.
Average book price: Free.
Additional Services: None.
Reply Time: ASAP

Submissions guidelines and procedures:

You must have written something! You must have finished what you have written. Uncompleted works will not be considered. You must make very sure that your work is ready to be published AS IS. You must send the completed work to BiblioBytes. If you are a previously unpublished author, you must supply them with an electronic file of your work; they will not publish your work otherwise. They recommend that you send electronic files, as they offer significantly higher royalties for electronic files; in addition, they can generally get electronic files online faster than paper manuscripts.

Make sure your cover letter includes your phone number, whether the work was previously published, other writing credits and any agent representation you use.

Do not send email submissions unless they have been approved, send query emails to submission@bb.com.

You must wait until they send you a contract and author's questionnaire. You must sign the contract and fill out the questionnaire completely. Then you must return them as quickly as possible.

The preferred word processor file format for electronic submissions is Microsoft Word. Font Palatino 12, paragraph indent .25 inches, no more than two blank lines. WordPerfect, WriteNow, MacWrite, RTF, and ASCII files are also accepted. Please query about other word processors or page layout programs. If you create HTML files yourself, email them for recommended specifications.

Send your work to:

BiblioBytes

71 Hauxhurst Ave.

Weehawken, NJ USA 07087-6803

Attn: Submissions

Book.mice.com e-Books
www.bookmice.com

Bookmice.com will market your e-book enthusiastically; their books are listed with Amazon, Barnes & Noble, Powell's and other online e-book sellers. The site dedicates a separate page to each author and offers comprehensive author profiles, synopses and extracts. Good art work too. They nominated a number of their authors for the First Annual International Ebook Awards.

Category: Fiction/Non-fiction.
Contact: Editor@Bookmice.com
Editor:
Royalties: 50%. Paid on a quarterly basis. Royalties of 30% of net retail sales (in US dollars) will be paid for the work, which is sold in CD, diskette or other physical mail-able format.
Rights: Electronic only.
Fees: None.
Contract: Term not stated.
Formats: PDF/ HTML /Palm formats/CD-ROM/Rocket e-Book.
Editorial Control: If they feel your manuscript is unacceptable for publication, they may recommend you edit the manuscript to make it more presentable and resubmit it.
Acceptance policy: They reserve the right to reject any manuscript which they feel is inappropriate, based on sloppy proof-reading, pornographic content, excessive violence or exceedingly bad writing. And you can't say fairer than that!
ISBN: None.
Average book price: PDF $5.95. HTML $5.95. CD $7.95. Palm $5.95.
Additional Services: None. •
Reply Time: 6-8 weeks.

Submissions guidelines and procedures:

1. Send complete manuscripts only.
2. Please do not send manuscripts on paper through the mail.

3. Ensure that you have proofread and spell-checked your manuscript.

4. Prepare the manuscript in a Word Perfect, Word or RTF file format in standard manuscript format (double-spaced, 1 inch margins, no "hard returns" at end of lines, no extra space between paragraphs, "hard page break" between chapters).

5. Please do not use the "space bar" to indent your paragraphs. Use tabs to indent.

6. Use only Arial or Times New Roman fonts.

7. Do not embed text in graphic boxes - place it within the text separated by two extra lines.

8. Do not use footnotes within chapters - place all footnotes at the end of the book with appropriate bracketed numbers in the text for reference.

9. If submitting by email, chapters must all be in one file (with hard "page break" between chapters).

10. Do NOT send ZIPPED/ compressed files

11. Prepare a covering email (or letter) including:

–your name (and pen name if any), address, telephone and email address

–brief synopsis describing the story or non-fiction subject

–the genre (if it's not obvious)

–word length

–brief details of your writing career (if it's your first book, tell us about your life!)

12. Send the manuscript as a file attachment to an email (NOT in the body of the email) addressed to: Editor@Bookmice.com

13. If you wish to submit by disk by mail it must be IBM compatible.

14. You will receive an immediate confirmation of receipt of your mss.

15. If accepted for publication, you will receive a contract by mail or via email.

16. You will also be notified of a publication date when your e-book will be listed on the website.

P.O. Box 1148, Sumas,
WA 98295-1148
Telephone: 604-850-1246 (9-5 USA Pacific Time Zone)

Booklocker.com
www.booklocker.com

Booklocker.com, Inc. is the parent company for the Booklocker.com and WritersWeekly.com web sites. Booklocker.com is their online book store and WritersWeekly.com is the resource centre through which they help writers make money online through self-publishing. Their 'Ebook Program' gives writers a place to sell their books as e-books. They will set up a 'book page' where you can refer your customers but they will handle the transaction and delivery of the e-book. They run a Print on Demand (POD) programme that allows them to print books one at a time as sales come in.

Category: Fiction/Non-fiction
Contact: angela@booklocker.com.
Editor: Angela Adair-Hoy.
Royalties: Pay 70% royalties on e-books costing $8.95 or more, 50% on lower priced e-books and 35% on print books printed using their Print On Demand programme. Pay royalties monthly.
Rights: Non-exclusive, which means you are free to sell your book elsewhere. Author retains all rights.
Fees: No sign-up fees. There are no costs as long as your book is ready for production. They charge $99.00 for the POD programme.
Contract: The contract is not exclusive and can be terminated at any time by sending them an email.
Formats: 95% of their e-books are in .PDF format, making them readable across all platforms (Macs and PCs).
Editorial Control: If they find more than a few mistakes in any book they will reject it, stating they can judge a books value and authors' efforts based on typos and grammatical errors. So beware.
Acceptance policy: They reject 70% of submissions.
ISBN: The writer can use an ISBN of their own or they can provide you with one through WritersWeekly.com.
Average book price: $8.95

Additional Services: Print on demand. Other services are offered through Writers Weekly.com: www.writersweekly.com.

Reply Time: 5 days or longer depending on their backlog.

Submissions guidelines and procedures:

Your book must be accepted for publication on Booklocker.com prior to being listed.

Once you receive a letter of acceptance, you will be provided with very detailed submission instructions.

Submit the following information by email to: angela@booklocker.com

You can cut and paste this information on the site into the text of an email:

1. Your name:

2. Your penname (if applicable):

3. Your email address:

4. Your web site URL (if applicable):

5. The title of your book:

6. Approx. number of pages your book will be after final formatting for e-publication:

7. Is your book already for sale anywhere besides Booklocker.com? (No, this does not hurt your chances of publication here, so don't worry.) If so, where?

8. Has your book been previously published in print?

9. If your book has already been published, either electronically or in print, please tell us approximately how many copies you have sold, combined (print and electronic):

10. Do you have an agent yet? (We need to know who to contact if a publisher requests your book.) If you do not have an agent, don't worry. We'll cross that bridge when we come to it. We have an agent that represents some books on Booklocker.com. And, no, there are no reading fees or any other fees involved whatsoever.

11. A sentence or two as to why you think your book belongs with us.

12. Do you publish an ezine/emag that targets your book's audience?

Finally, attach a text or MS Word file of your book to the email and click send.

Chapter & Verse
http://chapter-verse.com

Chapter & Verse provide electronic books of exceptional literary, artistic and cultural value to children from pre-Kindergarten age through high school. Their site is lovely, with engaging artwork and attractive fonts. Children will love visiting their pages.

Category: Children's Literature.
Contact: Editor@Chapter-Verse.com
Editor: Sarah E. Miano.
Royalties: 60/40 with the author/illustrator team.
Rights: Electronic rights only. Exclusive.
Fees: None.
Contract: Electronic rights are for the life of the copyright. No automatic release, but they are willing to negotiate a re-assignment of electronic rights if the creative team obtains a contract with a traditional publisher.
Formats: .PDF.
Editorial Control:
Acceptance policy: Between 10 and 12%, approximately.
ISBN: None.
Average book price: $7.95.
Additional Services: They put authors and illustrators together once a work has been accepted for publication. They also offer assistance on constructing self-promotion packages.
Reply Time: ASAP.

Submissions guidelines and procedures:

Manuscripts: If the text portion of the manuscript is "typed" then that portion of the manuscript should be submitted as a Microsoft Word file, or as an ASCII text file. Some works, particularly those for younger children, have only a few words or sentences per page. Please indicate pages either by formatted page breaks or by centred page numbers. Manuscripts should be submitted electronically as a file attachment to an email submission letter, the manuscript is hand-lettered, then it should be submitted in hardcopy. The cover letter should contain a brief overview of each work submitted, as well as a small biography of the author's professional or writing history. All manuscripts should have the author's name, mailing address and email address in the upper right hand corner of each page. If submitting manuscripts in hardcopy, please include a self-addressed stamped envelope for returns.

3528 Wade Avenue
PMB 139
Raleigh, NC 27607

Crossroads Publications

www.crossroadspub.com

Crossroads specialise in cross-genre and they are building a good reputation for the quality of their editing. Their sales are good and they publish books rapidly.

Category: Fiction.
Contact: CEO@crossroadspub.com
Editor: Sharon L Reddy.
Royalties: 50% of the sale price base of approximately $3.50 per copy.
Rights: Exclusive publication rights in electronic format.
Fees: None.
Contract: Twelve months from release date of a book in electronic format, with maximum duration of fifteen months from signing date.
Formats: Rocket eBook/HTML format.
Editorial Control: Each book they publish has been through a complete professional editing process; first read, story edit, second story edit, more story edits if needed, line edit and proofread.
Acceptance policy: Not stated.
ISBN: They will issue ISBNs for each format (HTML, Rocket, etc.) and binding (download, CD, etc.) of your book.
Average book price: $8.00.
Additional Services: Nominal set up fees for POD and audio books.
Reply Time: You'll know, usually within a few days, whether or not they want to see the full manuscript, and within less than two weeks if they want your book, and approximately how long it will be before an editor will start work on it.

Submissions guidelines and procedures:

Your legal name, pen name (if used) and contact information; email address and postal address. Their primary contact is email, so make sure that's correct.

Children's books:
  Send a query letter to ChildrenAQ@crossroadspub.com.

E-BOOK PUBLISHING

In the query/cover letter, include age of audience and expected number of illustrations. They must have this information to know what type of contract to send if your book is accepted. Include the entire text of books for small children, under 5,000 words, as an RTF attachment to the email. Attach the first three chapters in RTF format for books of greater length.

Books for mature or general audience:

Send a query letter to Acquisitions@crossroadspub.com

Include, title, brief (two or three paragraph) description, and first three chapters of the book in Rich Text Format (.rtf) as an attachment.

Target Market of the book. They want a description of your ideal reader; age, education level, etc. If your book is culture specific, if the slang or politics are too 'insider' for the international market, tell them. Upon request, send the entire book for editing in RTF (Rich Text Format).

The preferred font is "Times New Roman" 12-pt. Don't double space.

CrossroadsPub.Com
806 N Black
Silver City, NM, 88061
(505) 5334-1934

Crowsnest Books
www.computercrowsnest.com/greennebula/bkindex.htm

This web site is particularly forward thinking, see *'why most publishers suck & why evolution will happen…'* on the front page. The clubroom is password protected and available to Crowsnest authors only; it contains a number of resources for the writer, including Guerrilla, an online marketing guide, a private chat room and bulletin board.

Category: Science fiction/fantasy/horror/adventure/war/crime/thriller fiction
novels. They also publish non-fiction in the form of history, biographies, travel guides.
Contact: Commissioning Editor: gfwillmetts@REMOVEFORSPAMhotmail.com
Editor: G. F. Willmetts. Assistant Editor: Alex Larsen-Smith
Royalties: 40% on retail price on the first one hundred thousand copies sold and 50% thereafter.
Rights: Digital rights only.
Fees: None.
Contract: The Author grants to the Publisher for a period of ten (10) years from the date of first publication the sole and exclusive right to publish and sell an electronic version of the Work throughout the world.
Formats: Rocket eBook.
Editorial Control: Changes, additions, deletions, abridgements, or condensations in the text of the Work or changes of title may be made by the Publisher, its agents, or employees, with the consent of the Author which shall not be reasonably withheld.
Acceptance policy:
ISBN: Assigned.
Average book price: $5.00.
Additional Services: None.
Reply Time: ASAP.

E-BOOK PUBLISHING

Submissions guidelines and procedures:

Send your book synopsis and three sample chapters, along with a suitably priced stamped addressed envelope (SAE) for a reply - and manuscript return, if desired.

Should you live outside of the UK and wish to conserve post, mark your manuscript 'non-returnable' and send at least 2 International Response Coupons (IRCs) to cover our reply. These are available from your local post office in the US, Canada, Australia and Europe.

Samples and synopsis should be typed or printed on white paper. All page headers should contain the book title, your name and address, and have page numbers. The synopsis should be no more than 3 pages and also contain a potted history of yourself.

You should send your samples & SAE to:

Geoff Willmetts - Crowsnest Books
Commissioning Editor,
74 Gloucester Road,
Bridgwater,
Somerset TA6-6EA
UK

Dark Star Publications

www.darkstarpublications.com

Dark Star Publications is a good site for dark science and fantasy fiction writers. They have sister sites that take in several other genres, see www.pulsarbooks.com and www.starpublications.com. Check out those sites for details and submission guidelines. All sites are offering POD through Replica books.

Category: Dark Science Fiction/Fantasy
Contact: publisher@darkstarpublications.com
Editor: Terri Branson - Senior Editor
Royalties: 35%.
Rights: Electronic rights.
Fees: None.
Contract: One year, renewable.
Formats: PDF/e-reader (HTML) formats.
Editorial Control: Will suggest revisions.
Acceptance policy: All sites are looking for well-written material.
ISBN: The Publisher is responsible for obtaining the ISBN numbers.
Average book price: Download version $3.95. CD version $9.95
Additional Services: Print on Demand.
Reply Time: (4) weeks to three (3) months.

Submissions guidelines and procedures:

Send a cover letter, synopsis, and first chapter in the body of the email message, to publisher@darkstarpublications.com

Any unsolicited attachments to email will be deleted unread. All solicited files, however, are to be sent via email attachment in RTF (rich text format) for PCs in font Times New Roman, 12-point.

Dead End Street
http://deadendstreet.com

Dead End Street considers the work they publish to be outside the mainstream. They produce high quality literature across a broad range of genres. But they do offer alternatives to authors whose work is not yet of publishable quality by allowing them to post material in the Coffee Shop for which they charge a fee of $10.00. This includes a hyperlink directly to your personal email account, which allows for instant critique, criticism, input and feedback from hundreds of poets, authors and artists who visit the site.

Category: Fiction/Non-fiction
Contact: submissions@deadendstreet.com
Editor: Christine Mrazovich, Kristina Malensek, Jeff Conine, Michael McLellan, Amanda Lewanski.
Royalties: Completely negotiable, depending upon the quality and marketability of the respective work, and upon the authors following or lack thereof. As a general matter, 10-50%.
Rights: Exclusive license to produce and distribute the work.
Fees: None.
Contract: Query editor.
Formats: PDF and Rocket eBook.
Editorial Control: Material will be edited extensively.
Acceptance policy: 1-5%.
ISBN: Issued.
Average book price: PDF $5.99, Rocket eBook $10.99, print $14.95.
Additional Services: A nominal fee of $10 for each piece posted in the Coffee Shop.
Reply Time: ASAP.

Submissions guidelines and procedures:

A copy of the work should be sent to the Submissions Department for consideration. A staff editor is assigned to each work received. The staff editor performs a preliminary read to determine the readability and quality of the work, which is then either rejected or promoted to a second tier of review. If rejected, the author will be notified by email and your copy of the work will be destroyed (unless the author has expressly requested otherwise).

The second review of the work is intended to ascertain the editing required to render the work publishable. If the work is found to be of a high quality and readable, but requires serious editorial and/or structural changes before publication, the submission will be returned to the author with a cover letter detailing the changes/alterations requested. The work may then be resubmitted for expedited consideration after the requested changes/alterations have been made.

If the work is of a high quality, inherently readable, and requires relatively elementary editing or structural changes, the author will be sent a Notice of Acceptance by email (with a standard publication agreement enclosed). After the work is under contract, the author will be given a Publication Timetable and the substantive editing process will commence.

Work must be transmitted in either MS Word, WordPerfect, or RTF. Second, the work must be complete. Third, the work must have been vigorously proofread and relatively free of grammar problems. Fourth, include a 1-2 page synopsis of the work.

Dead End Street, LLC
813 Third Street
Hoquiam, WA 98550
Telephone:
206.817.4924

DLSIJ Press
www.dlsijpress.com

DLSIJ Press is a publisher and distributor of e-books by women authors.

Category: Fiction/Non-fiction.
Contact: dlsijpress@dlsijpress.com.
Editor: Sidney Jameson, Senior Editor.
Royalties: 40%.
Rights: Exclusive right to publish a work in electronic format.
Fees: None.
Contract: Two years.
Formats: PDF/Rocket/Palm. And a format for the sight-impaired.
Editorial Control: All contracted e-books will be edited prior to public availability.
Acceptance policy: Rigorous review process.
ISBN: Assigned at no extra cost.
Average book price: $4.95 - $19.95.
Additional Services: You will be required to file for your copyright, which requires a $20 filing fee and a hard copy of the manuscript.
Reply Time: They will acknowledge receipt of the material and they will contact you after the initial review.

Submissions guidelines and procedures:

Due to the volume of submissions they receive, they ask that authors query, rather than sending completed work. Please email the following to their editor or use their Upload Centre on site.

Query letter
Biographical statement
First three chapters
Fair representation of collection

Please name your files so that they reflect author name and title. Examples:
V_Woolf_Lighthouse.doc
V_Woolf_bio.doc
V_Woolf_query.doc

Completed work will be reviewed again. If it meets their standards, their editorial review board will decide upon the feasibility of a contract. All contracted e-books will be edited prior to public availability.

Dreams Unlimited
www.dreams-unlimited.com

Dreams Unlimited is a romance publisher, but they are looking for anything 'unusual.' They are not interested in formulaic romance. They are excellent at everything from editing to promotion, but they are very busy. In June 2000 they created a sister site for Historical and Contemporary romance, at www.daylight-dreams.com.

Category: Fantasy/Futuristic/Paranormal/Gay and Erotic Romance.
Contact: Editorial: editor@dreams-unlimited.com
Editor: Bonnee Pierson.
Royalties: 35% and up to 50% of the final (download) sales price. (i.e. if you are on a 50% royalty and your book sells for $5 off our site, you get $2.50 per sale.)
Rights: Electronic rights only.
Fees: None.
Contract: Rights are for six months and open to re-negotiation should the work sell well.
Formats: PDF format/ RocketBooks
Editorial Control: They will edit. Changes will only be suggested should they feel they are necessary. They do not publish on an 'as is' basis.
Acceptance policy: They have stringent requirements and are only looking for sub genre romance.
ISBN: Every book of ours has an ISBN with our publisher prefix assigned when it goes to contract.
Average book price: $5.00.
Additional Services: Cover art is commissioned by them.
Reply Time: They acknowledge submissions right away for receipt, so the turn-around is generally a day, no more than two. After request of a ms, the author gets a (secure) URL to check the status of the book, so that the number of emails can be reduced, as well as keeping everyone up to date.

Submissions guidelines and procedures:

Their main focus is hard-to-sell subgenre romances.

Telephone:
(++44) 07931 522974 (United Kingdom)
(++1) 203-484-9245 (United States)

Postal address:
21 Drummond Gardens,
Epsom, Surrey,
KT19 8RP, United Kingdom

PO Box 543,
Northford, CT 06472-0543,
United States of America

E-BOOK PUBLISHING

Ebooks on the Net
www.ebooksonthe.net

Ebooks on the Net have a good catalogue of books, and they have recently set up a new e-book club. The site is quite low-key but persuasive. It is not overloaded with information, however, but does provide print on demand services with distribution to most major bookstores, although authors are asked to pay their own set up fee. The contract is rather long in terms of the internet but they will give you early release under certain circumstances. Manuscripts are well edited, and carefully proofread.

Category: Fiction/Non-fiction.
Contact: C. Foster.
Editor: goodreading@ebooksonthe.net.
Royalties: 40%.
Rights: Non-exclusive rights only.
Fees: None, with the exception of POD. Authors who want their titles in print are asked to pay their own set up fee.
Contract: 2 years with early release if wanted.
Formats: HTML/PDB/PDF Ebook
Editorial Control: Manuscripts are proof read and edited.
Acceptance policy: Around 30%.
ISBN: Assigned.
Average book price: Download - $5.50. Paperback - $11.95.
Additional Services: Print on Demand, distribution to the major bookstores.
Reply Time: ASAP.

Submissions guidelines and procedures:

Works may be submitted by: Mail- a 3 1/2" MS/IBM compatible disc to:
C. Foster
PO Box 35
Ellsworth, Maine 04605

Or as an attachment in PDF, text or rtf by email to: goodreading@ebooksonthe.net

Ebook Express

http://www.m-pro.demon.co.uk

Ebook Express will publish anything on an 'as is' basis, you simply submit your work to them and they will display it. You set the price. Site also includes a book reviews section, a newsletter, interviews, a message board, and authors list.

Category: Fiction/Non-fiction.
Contact: Online contact available.
Editor: Chris J Randall
Royalties: 50% of the purchased price for each purchase made.
Rights: Author retains all book rights and may publish the covered work in other media and at other websites.
Fees: None.
Contract: Limited details.
Formats: HTML web pages and/or word text formats.
Editorial Control: M-pro do not read the full content of any book, but make their judgement of the standard of English and spelling on random paragraphs. They are not very much concerned with the content or story line, so will hardly ever consider this as a cause for rejection. However, this does not nullify their right to reject any book for whatever reason they decide. The decision of M-pro in this respect will be final.
Acceptance policy: They reserve the right to refuse publication of a book at the bookstore. Subject content would not generally be an issue as this amounts to censorship, but extremely poor use of language is unacceptable, as they do not expect their clients to pay for literary work which has little literary merit.
ISBN: None.
Average book price: Books sold for $4.95 - $9.95.
Additional Services: Will convert print books free of charge. Anything over 100,000 words, or in need of special formatting or graphics, will be assessed by them and charged for accordingly.
Reply Time: ASAP.

Submissions guidelines and procedures:

If your book is already on the web just send them your URL and tell them how much you wish to sell the book for and they will do the rest.

If your book is not on the web and exists as a text only document, you can send it to them by email and they will put it into the necessary format and add it to their bookstore website.

e-booksonline (UK) Ltd
www.e-booksonline.net/

"Inspirations and aspirations turned into reality."

This site is dedicated to producing previously unpublished work, out of print classics and books which the author feels should be made more easily available to the reading public. e-booksonline will publish any manuscript, subject to a few basic checks. The site is uncomplicated, with a good layout and it is very easy to find what you are looking for. Books for sale are divided into appropriate categories and include links to author bio's and extracts.

Category: General Fiction/Non-fiction
Contact: quillusers@cs.com
Editor: Directors: Arthur & Raie Wainwright. David & Mary Watson.
Royalties: 45% of the online price. Paid monthly.
Rights: All books available on these pages are held under copyright © from the author unless they are of such age as to be 'out of copyright'.
Fees: None.
Contract: Authors may withdraw their books with 28 days notice.
Formats: Microsoft's Word 97 format or higher.
Editorial Control: Some editing undertaken.
Acceptance policy: The company reserves the right to reject, without explanation, any manuscript or book, which is submitted to it. 99% acceptance rate.
ISBN: None.
Average book price: £3.50 for a downloaded book and £6.50 for a ring-bound printed book (postage included).
Additional Services: None.
Reply Time: ASAP.

E-BOOK PUBLISHING

Submissions guidelines and procedures:

Microsoft Word 97 or higher. They want on two floppy disks, the book, a synopsis (270 words), a sample (220 words), authors bio (125 words), snappy description (10 words) and if possible a coloured cover. No email submissions.

Plas Newydd, Rhoshirwaun, Pwllheli, Gwynedd, LL53 8HS U.K.
Telephone: 01758 760276 Fax: 01758 760602

email : home@e-booksonline.net
fax no : 01758 760602

Eboox (UK)
www.eboox.co.uk

Eboox.co.uk is relatively new to the e-publishing scene and at the time of writing this handbook they had no titles displayed. They have, however, been included because they make up a growing number of UK e-publishes that should be monitored in terms of progress and supported in their venture. This site tends to fall into the category of contract first, evaluation second, which seems to indicate that they are more inclined to accept manuscripts than reject them and this needs to be clarified by the writer before submitting to them.

Category: Fiction/Non-fiction. Young Adult, General and Children's as well as Health and Technology subsections.
Contact: angus.appleby@eboox.co.uk.
Editor: Angus Appleby (Editor) - Martin Rivett (Sub-editor)
Royalties: 50% royalties, per book sold, once every 6 months in arrears.
Rights: Electronic rights.
Fees: None.
Contract: Two-year period but you can withdraw your titles at any time.
Formats: PDF.
Editorial Control: Manuscripts must be free from grammatical and spelling errors.
Acceptance policy: As long as a book is deemed suitable they will put it up for sale.
ISBN: Not at this stage, due to their non-exclusive contract, but this could be an option should they wish to renegotiate with the author if they are insistent on having one.
Average book price: between £2.95 and £8.95 but always cheaper than a paperback equivalent
Additional Services: They will receive documents in any format but they make a £10.00 charge to convert them to PDF.
Reply Time: They try to review a book within 3 working days, if it needs editing it'll take longer, depending on amendments and discussions with the author.

Submissions guidelines and procedures:

Once you decide you want to register with them, click on the 'Submissions' button. This will take you to the registration form. Enter all information, and remember to check the acceptance button at the bottom of the page.

This will forward your contact information to them along with a copy of your acceptance of the contract. They will then email you a copy of the contract acceptance, along with a return email address for you to send your books, and a list of any other information they need. Once they receive your books attached to the email they will check them for errors and suitability and then offer them for sale in the e-store.

Electric eBook Publishing
www.electricebookpublishing.com

Their aim is to assist in the development of both new and emerging writers in all genres. They will work with any author who shows promise and are always available to give constructive feedback, editorial assistance, support and education. If they reject your novel you will get a reason why.

Category: Fiction/Non-Fiction/Poetry /Short Stories.
Contact: shannon.mobley@electricebookpublishing.com.
Editor: Shannon Mobley.
Royalties: For new unpublished manuscripts that are accepted for publication they pay 50% royalties. "Support The Writer" program which allows writers of short stories, poetry, and writing related articles to post their works for people to read. They pay the writers $.10 CAN for every person who reads their work.
Rights: The writer retains all rights to the work and by submission gives Electric eBook Publishing the right to post and display the work until notified otherwise by the writer.
Fees: None, although they do offer additional services.
Contract: No details.
Formats: HTML/PDF/WORD DOC.
Editorial Control: They work extensively with their authors.
Acceptance policy: All submissions will remain under consideration for a period of 6 months unless otherwise notified (For example, single poem submissions may be held for anthology consideration).
ISBN: Issued.
Average book price: $4.95US, $7.50CDN.
Additional Services: They offer print-on-demand services for their online customer base. Word Processing (includes spelling check) minimum 1 hour $20.00/hr. Proof Reading (Checks for typos, spelling, and grammar errors) $22.00/hr. Copy Editing (reads word by word and makes corrections and changes) $28.00/hr. Developmental Editing (assists with character, story-line, time-line, and continuity) $35.00/hr. Developmental Editing (assists with character, story-line, time-line, and continuity) $35.00/hr.

Reply Time: All submissions will be acknowledged upon receipt. Acceptance times vary, but are generally within 4 weeks. Publication within 6 months of acceptance.

Submissions guidelines and procedures:

Electric eBook Publishing considers manuscripts in the following genres:
•Adult fiction (all genres)
•Adult Non-fiction (all genres)
•Young Adult fiction
•Poetry (single poems and anthologies)

There are certain areas that they are eager to develop:

Canadian writers with Canadian themes. Previously unpublished authors. Modern stories that are universal in theme. Internet themes

Manuscripts may be submitted without prior authorisation. Submissions must not be with another publisher at present. They prefer email submissions, but will accommodate submissions via snail mail in paper or disk form (PC formatted). All submissions via the mail must include a self-addressed stamped envelope (SASE) for reply and/or return of the manuscript.

Email submissions should be sent as follows: subject header labelled as "Submission" files sent as an attachment in .PDF format or WordPerfect (.Doc) format contain a valid email address and author's name for contact purposes addressed to Shannon Mobley, Acquisitions Editor

Include a synopsis, three sample chapters and a brief author bio (including a list of previously published works if applicable).

Do not include any artwork unless you are a trained artist and never include original art.

Send all requests through our submission process.

Sending a Submission by Snail Mail

For those who wish to send a hard copy of their manuscript by regular mail here are the instructions:
• Enclose the manuscript in an appropriate covering with a return envelope with

adequate postage, a brief biography of you, a list of your previous works, a synopsis of the story you are submitting, and address the envelope to:

Electric eBook Publishing

Attention: Shannon Mobley, Acquisitions Editor

6254 Sycamore Street

Powell River, BC, Canada

V8A 4K9

• Be sure to include an email address for a faster response.

electricstory.com
www.electricstory.com

A publisher of new and reprint books in electronic form. All their editors and technical advisors have worked for top software and entertainment companies. They hope to branch out into thrillers, mysteries, mainstream and young adult books. They are one of the tougher markets to break into but if they like your manuscript they will help you develop your work. They have a free monthly newsletter, ES, which you can subscribe to via email, which provides updates on authors and information about their online community.

Category: Fantasy and science fiction but are also interested in mainstream, young adult and mystery titles.

Contact: submissions@electricstory.com

Editor: Robert P. Kruger, Publisher and Executive Editor. Lara Ballinger, Managing Editor.

Royalties: 50% net royalty, "net royalty" being defined as what they actually receive from the distributor, minus returns.

Rights: They lease exclusive, world wide electronic rights for three years, with an option to renew for another three-year term.

Fees: They assume all costs for production and promotion. An advance is not standard but is negotiable.

Contract: Three-year term. Can renew for another three-year term.

Formats: Rocket eBook, Microsoft Reader.

Editorial Control: Rigorous.

Acceptance policy: One of the tougher markets, especially in e-publishing, but they will work with an author to develop work if they're interested in it.

ISBN: None.

Average book price: All titles list for $7.99 but may be discounted at some stores.

Additional Services: None.

Reply Time: 6-8 weeks.

Submissions guidelines and procedures:

Manuscript Length: Books should be at least 50,000 words in length, 90,000 words, and up, preferred.

All submissions for original work should be sent via post, not email, and should include an SASE, query letter, sample chapter (or two stories if the work is a collection), and outline. If we are interested, we will require both a manuscript and electronic file of the work. To be considered for reprint, please submit a retail copy of the work, and be advised that if we are interested in republishing it and you are self-agented, we will need to review all previous publishing contracts before finalising an agreement.

Box 1126
North Bend, WA 98045

Electric Works Publishing
www.electricpublishing.com

Electric Works Publishing is very keen to promote socially responsible writing; they will not publish anything that promotes violence or gratuitous sex. They offer the first few chapters of a writer's book for free download, and there is a special page for Young Adult books. They are keen to promote new writers but are very selective in their choice of manuscripts.

Category: Fiction/Non-fiction
Contact: submissions@electricpublishing.com
Editor:
Royalties: 40% of the profit from the sale of your work.
Rights: They only ask for the digital publishing rights, so you can still have the work published elsewhere.
Fees: None. But they offer editing services, at a small percentage of the royalties.
Contract: Negotiable.
Formats: Digital format (e-books), these are all available in the HTML format and do not require a special "reader" device, in other words they will work with the same browser you are using right now. Some are also available in the "Open E-Book" format as well.
Editorial Control: In most cases, suggestions, acceptances or denials will be handled by the chief editor and emailed to you. You can place your work in the Electric Library without editing, provided it meets their guidelines.
Acceptance policy: Fairly selective.
ISBN: None.
Average book price: $4.50 - delivered through email, plus $1.50 to receive it on disk.
Additional Services: Editing services are available for 10% of the author's royalties.

If publishing rights to the work are assigned to another publisher, other than EWP, this fee follows the work . In other words, if EWP edits the work and a paper or other media publisher is found that will now accept the work, EWP will be entitled to 10% of the royalties due to the author/copyright holder from that publisher/producer.

Reply Time: ASAP.

Submissions guidelines and procedures:

If you submit anything to EWP, include your name, email address, and title of the work at the top of the first page of the work and in any correspondence.

The preferred method of submission is by email as an attachment.

To Submit your work for digital publishing: First, save the work as an RTF, (Rich Text Format), as a Word Perfect 8.0 or below, as a Word 97 or below document, or as a Works 4.0 or below document. Also make sure your email is not set-up for "quoted-printable" or "In-line". Graphics or cover art can be displayed in the Electric Library and can be included in the "primer", and the complete work. Do not send the illustrations through email until they have had a chance to look at the manuscript.

E-BOOK PUBLISHING

Electron Press
www.electronpress.com

They offer a very refreshing take on the world of e-publishing; they are interested in quality writing, rather than its commercial potential, and this is the key factor in the selection of their e-books.

Category: Fiction/Non-fiction.
Contact: editor@electronpress.com.
Editor: Philip Harris.
Royalties: 25 to 50%, completely dependent on the book, the author, etc. They tend to pay 25-35% for an unknown author's first work, and increase that by five or more percent each time for each subsequent work they publish, to a top of 50%.
Rights: Electronic rights only.
Fees: None.
Contract: Not listed.
Formats: Adobe Acrobat /Palm Pilot
Editorial Control: They undertake editorial revisions before they will publish the work.
Acceptance policy: Five percent of all submissions,
ISBN: None.
Average book price: $3.00 - $5.00
Additional Services: None. But they do edit, design and promote all the books accepted for publication.
Reply Time: In most cases they will respond within 2 weeks of the date they receive your query. Include your telephone number with your submission if you would like a voice response.

Submissions guidelines and procedures:

If you would like Electron Press to consider your book, submit an email query to editor@electronpress.com. Please attach a separate word processing file that contains the first two or three chapters (maximum 25 to 30 manuscript pages) of your book, preferably in Microsoft Word, WordPerfect, or RTF-format. They will review your proposal and sample, and let you know whether they would like you to send a printout of the entire manuscript.

If Electron Press decides to publish your book, they will send you a contract to review. When the contract signing is complete, you will have to provide the following items to Electron Press: The complete text of your book in a computer file (word processing or text file) on a standard 3.5" inch diskette. A one paragraph author's biography and (optional) portrait photo.

e-pulp
www.e-pulp.com

E-pulp encourages new writers but they also work with established writers. They pay above average royalties. Manuscripts are professionally edited by them at no cost to the writer. They have a very honest approach to e-publishing and do not make overblown claims to make you a best selling author, but they do believe in the industry and work hard for and on behalf of their authors. Bear in mind that basically your work has to be ready to go.

Category: Mystery/sci-fi/pop fiction
Contact: RDHynes@e-pulp.com.
Editor: R. Dalton Hynes, Senior Fiction Editor
Royalties: 85%.
Rights: Exclusive, world-wide, perpetual electronic rights.
Fees: None.
Contract: Electronic rights. If the author requests, they release them from the contact.
Formats: Rocket eBook.
Editorial Control: They will proofread and minimally-edit your ms, but they will not do heavy editing or rewrites.
Acceptance policy: Once you are under contract, their editorial staff will read your complete ms (manuscript.) Then they will either accept it and put it online, or they will return it and all rights to it. There are no charges for return of your rights if your completed ms is not accepted.
ISBN: Assigns.
Average book price: $4.95.
Additional Services: None
Reply Time: 30-60 days.

Submissions guidelines and procedures:

Send a plot outline (or chapter summary) and the first few chapters (not to exceed 30 pages) of your original work of fiction to the address below as hard copy, or electronically as a text file to the web site. If you are sending hard copy, include a self addressed stamped envelope for the return of your work. They have a strong preference for electronic copy, either on floppy disk or as a text file sent over the Internet. Their preferred word processing programs are Microsoft Word, ClarisWorks and Word Perfect.

If their editorial staff are interested in reading your complete manuscript, they will contact you and ask you to sign an author's agreement. They will not read your full manuscript until you have signed a contract with them. Once you are under contract, their editorial staff will read your complete ms (manuscript.) They will either accept it and put it online, or return it and all rights to it. Your work has to be ready to go.

Yellow Creek Publishing, LLC
P.O. Box 1261
Bath OH 44210

Gemini Books Inc
www.gemini-books.com

Lisa Schmitt founded the company in April 1999 with a vision of creating an outlet for mid-list, and cross-genre fiction authors and for small, niche technical, business and academic authors. They are committed to promoting literacy in schools and offer a number of services to the disabled community to allow access to their e-books, including voice synthesis technology, Braille printers and large text. If you have other special needs, let them know and they will try to accommodate you. They recognise the need to hear the voice of the 'unknown' author.

Category: Fiction/Non-fiction.
Contact: publisher@gemini-books.com.
Editor: Lisa Schmitt.
Royalties: The Author will receive 50% of all receipts for works that are purchased as email attachments or downloaded files. Royalties of 30% will be paid on all works that are sold in CD, diskette, or other mailable versions. Paid quarterly.
Rights: Electronic Publishing Rights.
Fees: None.
Contract: Two years. The contract may be terminated by the author with 90 days written notice to Gemini Books. If the contract is terminated prior to publication or within 12 months of publication Gemini Books will charge back to the author the expenses incurred in preparing the book for publication.
Formats: PDF/html/prc/rtf.
Editorial Control: Accepted submissions will be edited for grammar, spelling, punctuation, and content.
Acceptance policy: Not stated.
ISBN: None.
Average book price: CD - $9.75. Diskette - $8.70. Download - $4.00
Additional Services: None.
Reply Time: You will be notified when your manuscript is received with an approximate length of time before it can be reviewed.

Submissions guidelines and procedures:

Submissions should include the following:

Complete contact information for author (name, email address, postal address), title of work submitted, word count of completed manuscript (min. 40,000 words for novel-length works), a synopsis (not a chapter by chapter summary), and the first three chapters of the completed manuscript. Do not send chapters as individual files. Do not send complete manuscripts until requested.

Submissions may be submitted via email or USPS.

All submissions should be in one of the following formats: Microsoft Word (up to version 7.0), RTF, and html.

Submissions mailed via USPS should be on one of the following: CD, 3 _" diskette, or Zip100 disk.

If your work is accepted you can print off a copy of their contract from the site, fill in the blanks, sign it and return to their postal address.

P.O. Box 712
Trumann, AR 72472
fax: 870-483-1495
mail to: publisher@gemini-books.com

E-BOOK PUBLISHING

Hard Shell Word Factory
http://www.hardshell.com

Hard Shell is one of the early e-publishing companies online and has assumed a major role in setting standards for quality e-books and author friendly contracts. Since purchasing Hard Shell, Mary Wolf has expanded the line from about a dozen books to well over a hundred. Several Hard Shell books have won or been placed in writing contests and readers choice awards, including a finalist for best first novel in the International Horror Writers Guild Awards ("Dream Thieves"), and the winner of the 1998 Sapphire Award for SF Romance ("A Wizard Scorned"). Many Hard Shell authors placed in the top 25 in the 1998 Preditors and Editors Reader's Polls for best electronic novel. Hard Shell itself was voted #2 Electronic Publisher in the Universe in the same poll. Hard Shell was chosen as the only electronic publisher to be part of the Rocket eBook's list of Charter Publishers. They are also working with Librius and SoftBook Press as well as other e-reader companies to provide content in those formats.

Hard Shell Word Factory is one of the best known e-publishers on the internet.

They take a long time to read manuscripts and they only accept a very small percentage of submissions. Plus they don't really have time to encourage new authors' with potential. They accept cross genre, but nothing too 'way out'.

Category: Non-fiction/Fiction
Contact: books@hardshell.com Phone: (715) 824-5542 Fax: (715) 824-3875
Editor: Mary Z. Wolf, Publisher and Editor-in-Chief
Royalties: 30% of the $U.S. retail download price. Royalties on books sold at conferences, signings, etc, and in stores, either online or "physical": Author will receive 25% royalty of the net retail price.
Rights: Exclusive rights to publish and sell in readable (text) digital format (electronic download, disk, CD, E-Book.
Fees: None
Contract: Author's work is available for a full year with option for renewal. Contract can be terminated by the author or the publisher with a 90-day written, certified mail notice or other receipted delivery service.

Formats: E-reader and hand-held devices.

Editorial Control: They will undertake to edit manuscripts.

Acceptance policy: Not stated.

ISBN: The publisher will obtain ISBN's (International Standard Book Numbers) for the work, and will use the ISBN as part of the formal identification of the work.

Average book price: Publisher will set the retail price of the work, based on length and comparable works. Choice of downloadable formats: html, PDF $3.50 or disk, download $5.50.

Additional Services: None.

Reply Time: You can track progress of your submission by entering the log number you were given with your acknowledgement.

Submissions guidelines and procedures:

At the time of writing, submissions were closed, but this often happens and you must check the status of submissions on a regular basis.

The offices of Hard Shell Word Factory are located at:

PO Box 161, 8946 Loberg Rd., Amherst Jct. WI 54407

Phone: (715) 824-5542 Fax: (715) 824-3875 Email: books@hardshell.com

HotRead.com
www.hotread.com

HotRead.com has a good feel to it. The co-founders, Brett Williams and Susan Benton who are brother and sister, set up the business in 1999. They have strong beliefs and their main aims centre around the principle that many good writers are not given the exposure they need and readers are capable of recognising excellent writing when they see it. They showcase both established and new writers.

Category: Fiction/Non-fiction
Contact: info@hotread.com
Editors: Brett Williams and Susan Benton
Royalties: 40 cents per sale of the piece throughout posting. Payments will be made quarterly on or before April 30, July 31, October 30, and January 31.
Rights: Exclusive World Wide Web posting rights. Writer maintains complete copyright control and may submit to other publications freely.
Fees: Free.
Contract: After the "minimum contracted period" of posting, HotRead.com may A) continue to exclusively post your piece unless notified by you to remove it, or B) discontinue posting of your piece. If so notified by the author to remove the selection, the author will allow HotRead.com 7 days to complete this task.
Formats: rtf format.
Editorial Control: They will edit a manuscript until it is 'flawless', and will submit this to the author for approval.
Acceptance policy: Not stated.
ISBN: Not offered.
Average book price: $1.00
Additional Services: None.
Reply Time: 1 month.

Submissions guidelines and procedures:

Pieces should be 1,000-10,000 words, in English only. No erotica, pornography, extreme violence or graphic sex will be accepted. They do not publish books or poetry.

Submissions will be accepted by email only to Submissions@HotRead.com. In an email include your name, daytime and evening phone numbers, email address, and the word count of your selection. Please see formatting for rtf files here. Your manuscript will never appear in full on the web site. It can only be downloaded to the reader upon purchase.

Save your piece in Rich Text Format (.rtf) and attach it to your email or if you cannot attach rtf then copy and paste your story into email.

If you copy and paste do not forget to add blank lines between each paragraph or unformatted email will lose paragraph breaks. If you wish to expand the separation between paragraphs to represent a passage of time or space, separate the paragraphs with a series of four asterisks - "****". If your piece is selected, they will email a contract to you and ask you to return it along with: 1) your bio and 2) the category of fiction or non-fiction in which your story fits. You may or may not suggest a synopsis of 100 words or less and your preference of an excerpt of approximately 200 words. Submit only one piece at a time. Read at least one story to get an idea of what they expect.

HotRead.com
P.O. Box 2833
Iowa City, IA
52244
info@HotRead.com

New Concept Publishing
www.newconceptspublishing.com

New Concepts pay lower royalties than most, but they are extremely selective and their editing is second to none. They have been around for a long time and it seems they almost fall between being a print publisher and an e-publisher. They publish 6-10 novels a month. They now publish a variety of genre fiction and have recently released their first electronic children's book.

They are extremely dedicated to advertising their book list by participating in literary signings, book fairs, and trade shows. They use banner advertising to promote books along with newspaper interviews and press releases. They are currently focusing on the retail market and expanding their books into online bookstores as well as physical bookstores. They have recently landed a contract with Baker & Taylor distributors. The only problem with them is that it can take anywhere from six months to a year for them to put your book on line.

Category: Fiction/Non-fiction
Contact: ncp@newconceptspublishing.com.
Editors: Andrea DePasture, Editor - Futuristic, Fantasy, Science Fiction, Horror, and Paranormal. Madris Gutierrez, Editor - Historical, Time Travel, Young Adult. Jeri Smith, Editor - Contemporary, Suspense, Category (for Category Duets line) Margaret Wright, Acquisitions Editor - Mystery, Mainstream, non-fiction, children's, Nostalgia (1900-1979), Western, Thriller.
Royalties: One dollar for each disk or download sold directly through the site.
Rights: Only electronic rights for a specific period of time.
Fees: None.
Contract: Contract time is one to four years from time of publication, renewable. They are not keen for you to withdraw if they have invested heavily of their time and effort in a particular book.
Formats: Word/Wpwin/RTF/HTML.
Editorial Control: They spend a great deal of time making sure a manuscript is up to scratch.
Acceptance policy: The criteria for determining which books will be selected is

based upon the following guidelines: Originality - This could be a fresh new approach to a tried and true theme or something totally unique.

ISBN: They assign ISBNs once the contract is received and the book scheduled.

Average book price: Rocket $3.99. Disk = $3.99. Download = $3.50.

Additional Services: None.

Reply Time: About three to four months though sometimes longer if submissions are particularly heavy.

Submissions guidelines and procedures:

Please direct submissions to the appropriate editor.

Duets:

This is the pairing of two category-sized novels (50,000-69,000 words) into one volume either by two different authors or both by the same. Royalties are split equally between the author(s) and NCP.

Nostalgia:

Nostalgia can be romance, mystery, horror or other sub-genres but the element which makes these novels compare is the time-frame of the books. Any novels set between 1920 and 1979 apply.

Submission Guidelines

One (1) printout of manuscript—Standard Format - The manuscript must be double spaced with one (1) inch margins top, bottom and sides. The right margin of the text should not be justified. The page number, author's name and title of book should appear at the top of each page. We do not have very stringent word count requirements. We would not consider anything under 60,000 unless it was to be published as a pair of novellas together in one volume.

You should include with your submission, one (1) SASE large enough to accommodate the return of your manuscript after it has been reviewed.

Once your manuscript has been edited and is considered professionally polished, you will be asked to submit your finished manuscript in disk form. You will need to provide NCP with a short biography, which outlines your credentials and/or contains some personal information about yourself readers might find of interest. You will also be required to submit a `blurb' of the book, the book's genre or sub-genre and rating, and a short excerpt of your book.

E-BOOK PUBLISHING

No electronic submissions, send manuscripts to:
4729 Humphreys Road
Lake Park, Georgia
31636
US

Phone: (912) 257-0367
Fax: (912) 257-0366

NiteLinks

www.nitelinks.com

Founded in 1977, Nitelinks run a pretty slick operation; they are committed to customer services and expect high standards from their authors. Has good feedback links; anything nice said about an author will be emailed to them. Author bios are available along with extracts of books.

Category: Fiction/Non-fiction
Contact: President@NiteLinks.com or query@nitelinks.com
Editor: Laura Higley.
Royalties: Remuneration is a sliding-scale royalty of 10% to 40% based on gross sales.
Rights: World Wide Web Internet rights.
Fees: Nitelinks, Inc.'s publishing service is free to authors.
Contract: Standard publishing contract, but it also includes an "out" clause if a paper publisher wishes to publish the work. This enables writers, if they choose, to pursue traditional publication before the contract expires.
Formats: CD ROM/Download via NSR. NSR (Nitelinks Story Reader) is required to read their books; this software is available for download from the site. NSR protects the author copyright of the books they sell.
Editorial Control: They do not undertake major editing. If a submission contains more than a reasonable number of editorial and technical errors, they will not publish it.
Acceptance policy: They look for books consistent with the level of quality they have established for the company.
ISBN: Not offered.
Average book price: $5.95 download, $8.95 CD-ROM
Additional Services: None.
Reply Time: They respond to all submissions as soon as possible. While this may take up to three months (12 weeks,) they do their utmost to respond to all submissions within six weeks.

E-BOOK PUBLISHING

Submissions guidelines and procedures:

They encourage all writers first to send them a query letter and SASE, describing the work briefly and concisely. However, Nitelinks, Inc. currently accepts unsolicited manuscripts. Multiple (or "simultaneous") queries are encouraged. Do not query unwritten or incomplete works.

Include the following information: Date; Application; submitted by: Author name. Address, City, state, zip code. Phone, fax, email. Title of work. Genre. Has this work been previously published? If so, list publisher's name & indicate if self published. Length of work (in words, not pages). Completion date. Agent name (Optional). Agent address. Agent city, state, zip code. Agent phone, fax, email. Send inquiries to agent or author? Other published works by author.

Submissions are preferred on IBM or Windows compatible 3.5" floppy disk, in ASCII .TXT format. The disk should be accompanied by a cover letter, synopsis, and self-addressed, stamped envelope (SASE.)

Paper submissions are discouraged.

Diskette submissions are preferred. Consider paper submissions a last resort, and only send those typed neatly on 81/2" x 11" paper and double-spaced with 1 1/2" margins on all sides. Query letters are customarily single-spaced. Photocopies and printed submissions must be clear and letter quality. They will reject any illegible submission.

Snail Mail
Nitelinks, Inc.
P.O. Box 41
Haskell, NJ 07420

Telephone
973-831-1263

Online Originals

http://www.onlineoriginals.com

Online Originals is UK based and produced Patricia Le Roy's The Angels of Russia, the first Booker Prize nominated e-book. They have also published her sequel, Music at the Garden House. Frederick Forsyth has also published an e-book series with them. They operate exclusively on the Internet, and have a team of very skilled editors and reviewers who select material carefully. The site is extremely well organised both for potential readers and authors. Descriptions and sample chapters are available of all titles published. They provide a number of resources for authors including the chance to have a manuscript "peer reviewed". They have a growing interactive writing community, which allows authors and readers to exchange information. Authors are advised to undertake additional promotion of their individual titles for maximum exposure and they offer a number of "Writers' Services" to guide the author. Online Originals are one of the big players in the e-book industry, they have a strong list of authors and their editorial control and selection process is rigorous, which means they produce good quality content. The price of their e-books may seem high but author royalties are also high, and authors should expect to sell e-books through them. They exude a confidence that should settle the stomachs of authors who are wary of considering e-publishing as an option and obviously, with the addition of some heavy duty authors climbing on board, they look set for a rosy future.

Category: Non-fiction including academic works, as well as fiction and drama for both adults and younger readers.
Contact: editor@onlineoriginals.com
Editor: Chris Macann
Royalties: 50% royalty on all titles they sell.
Rights: Worldwide electronic.
Fees: None.
Contract: Proofs/editions vary.
Formats: Palm/PDF/Rocket eBook/Microsoft Reader
Editorial Control: Rigorous editorial procedure.

Acceptance policy: They offer constructive feedback on all submissions, and a review system. Runs at 5%.

ISBN: Issued.

Average book price: Each 'Proof' work you order costs only $7 (US dollars), equivalent to £4 (pounds) or 7 Euro. Editions cost only $10 or £6, equivalent to 10 Euro.

Additional Services: To maximise potential readership, authors can commission Online Originals to convert their titles into extra formats. For one extra format: £60 ($100) For two extra formats: £100 ($160). Authors can commission reviews of their work by a member of their team of reviewers for a fee of £60.00.

Reply Time: 1 month.

Submissions guidelines and procedures:

All Online Originals books must meet five basic requirements. Each work must be book-length. It must not be published already in any form (not even on the Internet). It must also be original in the sense that it expresses new ideas. It must be well-written and intelligent. And it must be available in digital form in English or French.

Before you make a submission enquiry, examine their editions. Read the sample chapters and a sample of their complete works. If you believe your work is strong enough for their list they have an online form that you can complete. You can look at their technical FAQ's on site.

Send them your synopsis and they will take care of the rest. You can visit www.onlineoriginals.com/howto.html, and they will be happy to send you a copy of their submission guidelines.

Online Originals,
6th Floor, Charter House,
2 Farringdon Road,
London, EC1M 3HP

Do not send manuscripts to this address

Virtual Book.com
www.virtualbookworm.com

They offer a virtual host of services, most at a fee. They have a number of e-publishing and print publishing programmes that you can take advantage of, but their prices are fairly steep and if you do, then it is going to cost you. However, if your book is 'ready to go' there are no charges.

Category: All genres.
Contact: publish@virtualbookworm.com
Editor: Bobby Bernshausen.
Royalties: 50% on a 'ready to go' e-book. Other royalties vary depending on choice of 'package'.
Rights: Non-exclusive.
Fees: Publishing fees range from $25.00 to $400.00 for complete package.
Contract: Their contracts are for two years, but they always give authors the opportunity to be released from the contract upon approval of a 90-day written notice.
Formats: .PDF format
Editorial Control: They review the manuscripts to make sure they meet their guidelines. They will edit the works at times for clarity, etc. They do not proof the manuscripts, however they do offer such services for as little as $100.
Acceptance policy: They reserve the right to refuse any manuscript for any reason.
ISBN: Optional.
Average book price: $2.50 for download.
Additional Services: Professional cover: Starting at $90. Copyediting/Proofing: Starting at $200. Copyright Procurement: $39 plus filing charges. Library of Congress Number: $50. E-book preparation: With the purchase of any POD package, you can have your book set up for e-book distribution with all of the contents of the "Goin' Digital Package" (Package 3) for only $25 extra. Personal website: $72 for one year, $130 for two years, $175 for three years (although once the site is set up maintenance is up to you.) POD for $99.00.
Reply Time: One week.

Submissions guidelines and procedures:

They have an online submission form to fill in, then, within 24 hours of that submission, email a query letter that contains your title, a brief description of your book and two sample chapters. The email should also contain your legal name and pen name, as well as your email and postal address. Your phone number isn't required, but they do like to contact new authors personally upon acceptance (when time permits). List a URL address if you currently have a web site.

If you would like to contact them, email:

Advertising: sales@virtualbookworm.com

Publishing: publish@virtualbookworm.com

Problems: webmaster@virtualbookworm.com

Additional Questions: info@virtualbookworm.com

Wordbeams.com
www.wordbeams.com

This is a mother and daughter team. They provide a good collection of e-books and have a lot of talented authors on site. There is a facility for readers to submit a 'reader review' on the site, and a free newsletter entitled 'Beamings'. They actively promote their authors' books through a variety of marketing channels, but they encourage individual authors to promote their work themselves. They also offer a number of resources for writers to brush up on their writing technique.

Category: Fiction/Non-fiction.
Contact: submissions@wordbeams.com.
Editor: Susan Bodendorfer, Publisher. Jen Bodendorfer (Senior Editor)
Royalties: 35% of the U.S. retail download price.
Rights: Electronic rights.
Fees: None.
Contract: One-year period. After one year, rights are open to re-negotiation should your work sell well. Contract may be terminated by either the Author or the Publisher with a ninety-day written notice sent by certified or other delivery in which a receipt is provided.
Formats: Microsoft Word/RTF/WordPerfect 5 or any other format agreed upon by the Author and Publisher.
Editorial Control: They edit each accepted manuscript.
Acceptance policy: Their goal is to publish, innovative, original stories, told with a fresh voice and executed with top-quality, professional writing skills.
ISBN: The Publisher will obtain appropriate ISBN's (International Standard Book Numbers) for the Work and will use the ISBN as part of the formal identification of the Work.
Average book price: $7.75 diskette, $4.95.
Additional Services: None.
Reply Time: ASAP.

E-BOOK PUBLISHING

Submissions guidelines and procedures:

Times New Roman 12 point (or similar serif font as substitute). 1" margins all around Ragged right (do not justify margins!). Single spaced—no extra return between paragraphs. Indent paragraphs using TABS, NOT the space bar or paragraph format codes. Headers: Use headers ONLY if you are formatting in MS Word. Headers should contain Title, Author and page number. Chapters: Indicate a new chapter with a hard page break at the bottom of the last page of each chapter. Skip 2 or 3 spaces, centre, and type the chapter name in bold 16 pt. title case text. End the manuscript with "the end" or "end" Your chapters should all be together in ONE file. Do NOT make a separate file for each chapter.

Length: Total word count should ideally be between 50,000 to 150,000 (anything shorter may be considered for a short story anthology or for a pair of novellas published together in one volume — anything longer than 150,000 words may be submitted, but files can't be too large or they'll take forever for readers to download).

Save in Microsoft Word (preferred) [do NOT use macros], or RTF (Rich Text Format). RTF files must have the ".rtf" extension. If you can't save your work in one of these formats, email us to see if we can accept your format. Name your file either the title of your story or use your last name. Do NOT name your file "submission." Also, be sure to put your name and email address on the first page of your manuscript along with the title of your book.

Write a professional cover letter. Your cover letter must include:
Your real name (not just your Internet handle or screen name)
Your home address
Your home telephone number
Your email address
Title of your manuscript
Your pseudonym (pen-name) if using one Genre/Sub-genre/Subject (or one sentence description of the work), such as - Paranormal or Contemporary Romantic Comedy or Historical Romance with strong elements of Mystery/Suspense, etc.
Word Count
A brief (no more than 150 words) thumbnail sketch of your story line (or subject for non-fiction—and YES, this is in addition to the synopsis). Your writing back-

ground (including publishing credits if any) Operating system used (Windows 98, 95, 3.1, Mac, etc.) Word processing program and version used (MS Word 2000, WordPerfect 5.1, etc.) Whether this is a simultaneous submission (and if so, to which other publishers). Simultaneous submissions are permitted ONLY if you inform us in your cover letter. We expect the author to have the courtesy to notify us IMMEDIATELY if the story has been accepted for publication elsewhere

Synopsis/Outline:

Fiction: Include a short (2 to 4 page), double spaced synopsis, describing the entire story (highlighting conflict and resolution) in a clear and concise manner. This is not the time to do a cliff-hanger — your synopsis must describe the beginning, middle and end of your story. Non-fiction: Include a detailed chapter-by-chapter outline rather than a synopsis Children's Picture Books: Include a short synopsis and a couple of sample illustrations if you have them. Also, indicate the targeted reader's age and/or grade range.

Email submissions to: submissions@wordbeams.com.

Wordbeams
Submissions Department
P. O. Box 23415
Portland, OR 97281-3415

World Wrangler Publishing Inc
www.worldwrangler.com

Word Wrangler Publishing was created by Barbara Quanbeck and Lesley Ehrhart to bring authors an affordable and quality means of publishing and selling their writing in a readily-accessible format. Barbara Quanbeck has been writing for over 30 years. Published in both prose and poetry, she possesses a strong background in the English language, including the areas of editing and language usage. Lesley Ehrhart is originally from Oxford, England and has been published in both prose and poetry. Before coming to America, Lesley spent sixteen years at Oxford University Press. Altogether, they make a pretty impressive team.

Category: Fiction /Non-fiction
Contact: WrdWranglr@aol.com.
Editor: Barbara Quanbeck and Lesley Ehrhart
Royalties: fifty percent (50%) of the retail price (attached file, diskette, CD) in US Dollars (USD) on all sales as long as they are sold through WWP or a WWP-approved vendor. This does not include discounted sales to the author. Royalties will be paid quarterly.
Rights: Electronic rights only. You maintain the right to publish or self-publish in print.
Fees: Free
Contract: 12 months. Either party may terminate this agreement at any time with or without cause upon 30-day notice.
Formats: Authors' e-books will be made available as email attachments or via snail mail on floppy disk. Word Wrangler creates and publishes eBooks in HTML.
Editorial Control: Word Wrangler does make small editing corrections on polished manuscripts at no charge.
Acceptance policy: Not stated.
ISBN: While it is not necessary for you to have an ISBN to be listed with them, they would prefer that you do.
Average book price: e-book - WWP $8.95 HTML, Win 95/98 (email attachment). E-book - WWP $10.95 HTML, Win 95/98 (floppy disk).

Additional Services: Editing service - $20.00 an hour.
Reply Time: Four to six weeks after receiving your submission.

Submissions guidelines and procedures:

Email attachments or snail mail submissions on disk are acceptable.

Please include: Complete manuscript/Single spaced/No Footer /Title of the manuscript in the header /All underlined words or phrases changed to italics

Please write the following on the cover page in the upper left hand corner:
Author's Name
Author's Address
Author's Phone Number
Author's FAX Number, if available
Author's Email Address
Title of Manuscript
Byline
Genre/Subgenre
Word Count (limit of 200,000 words in novels)

Submit between 35 and 60 poems; between 10-50 short stories. Novels should number no more than 200,000 words.

Email submissions should not be in the body of the email. Please send them as an attachment to email or on diskette. Chapter or page number should be centred at the top of the first page of each chapter or page. A hard page break should be at the bottom of the last page of each chapter. For ease of reading, use Arial 12. Please do not use HTML.

Acceptable Submission Formats: Microsoft Works /Microsoft Word /Word Perfect 6.0 or above /Rich Text Format /DOS Text

Please send electronic submissions to: WrdWranglr@aol.com.

Snail mail submissions may be sent to:
Word Wrangler Publishing
332 Tobin Creek Road
Livingston, Montana 59047

Zander ebooks
<u>www.zanderebooks.com</u>

Zander Publications is also a royalty-paying e-publisher. They are actively seeking new authors to represent on the site. They offer a number of services to their authors, including a password so that you can log into the 'Authors Only' area, which really does contain a lot of information that will help you. Their standard marketing package is free for each title you publish with them.

Category: Fiction/Non-fiction/Children's.
Contact: info@zanderebooks.com.
Editor:
Royalties: 70% royalties on the list price of e-books that are 50,000 words or more in length, and 50% royalties for books with fewer than 50,000 words. Payments are made on a quarterly basis.
Rights: For the first 6 months after publication, you agree to grant them exclusive rights to list and sell your work.
Fees: None.
Contract: After the 6 months are up, authors are free to list and sell their work anywhere.
Formats: PDF, SoftBook, Rocket eBook, HTML, PDF, OEB, and MS Reader.
Editorial Control: They evaluate manuscripts based on their literary merit, quality of information, quality of writing style, creativity, and overall professionalism.
Acceptance policy: Currently running at about a 38% acceptance rate.
ISBN: See services
Average book price:
Additional Services: Zander Publications provides several services to authors, including document conversion, cover art creation, and ISBN procurement.
Reply Time: ASAP

Submissions guidelines and procedures:

Your e-book can be initially submitted as a Microsoft Word, WordPerfect, PDF, RTF, or ASCII (TXT) document. However, Microsoft Word is the preferred format. Graphics must be submitted as a GIF or JPEG file, and should be no larger than 15K. This can vary slightly.

1. Proofread and spell-check your manuscript. 2. In the body of an email message, include: The title of your book & a short synopsis. Approx. # of pages your book will be after final formatting. A sentence or two as to why you think Zander eBooks should publish your work. 3. Attach your manuscript to the email message. They recommend it be in Microsoft Word format, so that they can convert it to OEB and SoftBook formats as well as PDF, but they will accept submissions in WordPerfect (PC), PDF, RTF, or ASCII (Text only, .TXT) format. Combine your chapters and attach as one file. 4. Send it to manuscripts@zanderebooks.com. This is a special, dedicated email address that they have set up specifically for manuscript submission. If your manuscript file is larger than 5MB in size, let them know, they will make other submission arrangements with you. 5. You will receive a confirmation email and a submission number. Please keep this number and include it in all future correspondence with them.

E-BOOK PUBLISHING

Zeus Publications
http://www.zeus-publications.com

Zeus Publications Australia is a privately owned family business. It was Australia's first e-book publisher and online e-bookshop. General Manager Bruce Rogers is experienced in all facets of the publishing industry and is a qualified graded Journalist with over 20 years experience in the media in marketing, sales, promotion, management and production. Provides extract of work, synopsis and author bio on sales pages.

Category: Fiction, non fiction, romance, children's, science fiction, self help, religious and many other genres except pornography.
Contact: zeus@omcs.com.au
Editor:
Royalties: 30% on all retail sales.
Rights: Electronic publishing rights only; the author retains print rights.
Fees: An author whose work has been submitted for consideration, or accepted for publication, will never be charged any fees, unless extensive editing and rewriting is required.
Contract: Not published.
Formats: HTML. Rocket eBook. Text format.
Editorial Control: Undertake minor editing.
Acceptance policy: They reserve the right to reject any submission.
ISBN: Assigned.
Average book price: All prices are in Australian dollars - the book prices range from $6.00 to $10.00 (about $3 to $6 US dollars and £2 to £4 GBP).
Additional Services:
Reply Time: It may take several weeks before they contact you with their initial response.

Submissions guidelines and procedures:

The work must be original and one to which the author holds the copyright. It must not be encumbered by any previous contractual obligations to a third party. Send in the first instance:

1   A one page query letter
2   A concise synopsis.
3   A representative sample of the work: · The first three chapters of a work or three representative short stories from a book-length short story collection or three representative essays from a book-length collection of essays.

They will acknowledge the receipt of the work and then contact you with their initial response. Provide them with an email address and a phone number. If you have mailed them a disk, please provide a SASE with your submission. If your work meets their criteria and current publishing needs, they will request a copy of the complete work. Please do not submit a complete work unless requested to do so. Once they have reviewed the complete work, they will notify you of their decision regarding publication.

All submissions, both initial queries and complete works, should be in an electronic format. The work should be a file in Word, WordPerfect, or RTF format. It should be submitted on a floppy disk, or as an email attachment(s). Only PC format is acceptable, formatted with one-inch margins all around and edited for spelling and grammar to the best of the author's ability. If you are sending your initial query as an email attachment please send it to: zeus@omcs.com.au

If you are mailing a disk, send it to: Zeus Publications Australia, P.O. Box 2554, Burleigh MDC Qld. 4220 Australia.

E-BOOK PUBLISHING

1st Books
http://www.1stlibrary.com/

They offer an impressive number of services, but at a price. They produce a 1st Books catalogue, which lists more than 4,000 titles, and selected books are available in paperback. Electronic books can be re-formatted for distribution in soft cover from all bookstores and distributed by Ingram Book Group. Ingram supplies bookstore chains such as Barnes & Noble and Amazon and supplies 25,000 bookstores in the US and 1,700 abroad. The soft cover versions come with a four-colour cover and perfect binding and to keep productions costs to a minimum they are produced on demand. They are currently running a 1st Books Award Program. If you are the top combined seller of e-books, Rocket eBooks, and printed and bound books (based on quantity sold according to the 3rd and 4th quarterly reports), they will write you a cheque for $20,000, first runner-up gets $10,000 and runner-up gets $5,000.

Category: Fiction/Non-fiction.
Contact: Uses on line forms.
Editor: Timothy Jacobs, President.
Royalties: 100% for first $300, 40% thereafter, 30% on print version
Rights: You retain all rights to your book. This means (1) that you are free to publish elsewhere at any time and (2) that you could possibly sell the rights to your book to be made into a Hollywood movie.
Fees: There is a one-time set up deposit of $159 plus a returnable deposit of $300. Total investment: $459 but could rise to $1,500 if all services are used.
Contract: Worldwide Distribution Agreement.
Formats: 1st Book, Rocket eBook.
Editorial Control: Editing and proofreading are the responsibility of the author.
Acceptance policy: They accept most submissions (currently 91%).
ISBN: Planned. Also offer a print on demand trade paperback service with links to Ingram.
Average book price: In general, they price electronic books at about fifty to seventy-five percent of what readers pay for soft cover books in conventional bookstores.

Additional Services: Paperback versions costing an additional $450, and hardback editions for $350 more. These allow ISBN and listing in 'Books in Print' at Ingram. They also offer a variety of promotional and editing services.
Reply Time: ASAP.

Submissions guidelines and procedures:

You may submit your manuscript in a number of ways. However, submitting books on disk gives authors more direct control of appearance and content. To insure that readers receive exactly what you want, they strongly suggest you submit your book on a disk in any of the following standard formats: 1. Microsoft Word for Windows (Macintosh versions are also acceptable) 2. Files saved in "Rich Text Format" (Macintosh versions are also acceptable) Note to Mac users: Please output to IBM disk format if possible!

1. Submit your book as a single file, including the title page, table of contents (if any), all of the chapters and index (if any). In many cases, page numbers, headers, indexes, and tables of contents are not necessary since most modern word processors used by readers automatically assign page numbers and search for key words. Usually, 600 to 700 pages will fit on one disk.

2. You may submit your "About the Author" and "About the Book" segments as separate files. (If you decide to submit these items on paper, please make sure you write clearly and say exactly what you want.) Remember the purpose of these items is to convince a reader to buy your book.

3. They will give your readers a two or three page "Free Preview."

1st Books will accept paper manuscripts. They will scan your manuscript and convert it to computer format so that it can be installed in the library for a fee of $2.25 per image scan or page. Scanning errors are corrected free of charge but other changes (unrelated to scanning) are charged at the rate in effect at the time of change (currently this is $60 per hour). Naturally, because of the additional steps involved, it takes slightly longer to prepare hard-copy manuscripts for online publication.

Use the Submission Agreement or a separate sheet to clearly tell readers "About the Book" and "About the Author." Also include what pages to show readers for the "Free Preview" section.

E-BOOK PUBLISHING

1stBooks Library
2511 West Third Street
Bloomington, IN 47404 USA
800-839-8640 (Toll Free)
812-839-6000 (Outside USA and Canada)
812-339-6554 (Fax)

Quick Guide to Royalty Payments

AGoodBook.com

www.agoodbook.com

Royalties: 20% of the selling price for all copies sold, less a reserve for credit card disputes. Initially, this reserve will be 10% of royalties and will be adjusted up or down based on actual, documented experience. Accounting for royalties will be made monthly, on the 25th of each month, for the preceding month.

Allandale Online Publishing

www.allandale.co.uk

Royalties: 1.A flat rate of 30% of the net receipts on every ebook sold. 2.A flat rate of 30% of the net receipts after 100 ebooks have been sold.

ArtemisPress

www.artemispress.com

Royalties: 40% of the U.S. retail download price. 40 percent on outside sales made through online distributors, bookstores and other organisations.

Authors Online

www.authorsonline.co.uk

Royalties: 60% net of the retail price, paid monthly.

Avid press LLC

www.avidpress.com

Royalties: 30% in US$ of the retail download price. 10% of net received on print versions.

Awe-Struck E-books

www.awe-struck.net

Royalties: 40% paid quarterly.

Bookbooters

www.bookbooters.com

Royalties: In addition to the 25%-50% you earn on all e-book sales of your novel, you will earn 25% on the net profits of paperback sales. Cheques will be mailed to the author no later than the third working day of each calendar month.

BiblioBytes

www.bibliobytes.com

Royalties: BiblioBytes pays a royalty on revenues realized from sales of 35%, which may be amended from time to time by mutual agreement. Royalty statements are computed quarterly on March 31, June 30, September 30, and December 31 of each year.

Book.mice.com e-Books

www.bookmice.com

Royalties: 50%. Paid on a quarterly basis. Royalties of 30% of net retail sales (in US dollars) will be paid for the work, which is sold in CD, diskette or other physical mail-able format.

Booklocker.com

www.booklocker.com

Royalties: Pay 70% royalties on e-books costing $8.95 or more, 50% on lower priced e-books and 35% on print books printed using their Print On Demand programme. Pay royalties monthly.

Chapter & Verse

http://chapter-verse.com

Royalties: 60/40 with the author/illustrator team.

Crossroads Publications

www.crossroadspub.com

Royalties: 50% of the sale price base of approximately $3.50 per copy.

Crowsnest Books

www.computercrowsnest.com/greennebula/bkindex.htm

Royalties: 40% on retail price on the first one hundred thousand copies sold and 50% thereafter.

Dark Star Publications

www.darkstarpublications.com

Royalties: 35%.

Dead End Street

http://deadendstreet.com

Royalties: 10-50%.

DLSIJ Press

www.dlsijpress.com

Royalties: 40%.

Dreams Unlimited

www.dreams-unlimited.com

Royalties: 35% and up to 50% of the final (download) sales price. (i.e. if you are on a 50% royalty and your book sells for $5 off our site, you get $2.50 per sale.)

Ebooks on the Net

www.ebooksonthe.net

Royalties: 40%.

Ebook Express

http://www.m-pro.demon.co.uk

Royalties: 50% of the purchased price for each purchase made.

e-booksonline (UK) ltd

www.e-booksonline.net/

Royalties: 45% of the online price. Paid monthly.

Eboox(UK)

www.eboox.co.uk

Royalties: 50% royalties per book sold, once every 6 months in arrears.

Electric eBook Publishing

www.electricebookpublishing.com

Royalties: For new unpublished manuscripts that are accepted for publication they pay 50% royalties. Pays the writers $.10 CAN for every person who reads their work.

electricstory.com

www.electricstory.com

Royalties: 50% net royalty, "net royalty" being defined as what they actually receive from the distributor, minus returns.

Electric Works Publishing

www.electricpublishing.com

Royalties: 40% of the profit from the sale of your work.

Electron Press

www.electronpress.com

Royalties: 25 to 50%, completely dependent on the book, the author, etc. They tend to pay 25-35% for an unknown author's first work, and increase that by five or more percent each time for each subsequent work they publish, to a top of 50%.

e-pulp

www.e-pulp.com

Royalties: 85%.

Gemini Books Inc

www.gemini-books.com

Royalties: The Author will receive 50% of all receipts for works that are purchased as email attachments or downloaded files. Royalties of 30% will be paid on all works that are sold in CD, diskette, or other mailable versions. Paid quarterly.

Hard Shell Word Factory
http://www.hardshell.com

Royalties: 30% of the $U.S. retail download price. Royalties on books sold at conferences, signings, etc, and in stores, either online or "physical": Author will receive 25% royalty of the net retail price.

HotRead.com
www.hotread.com

Royalties: 40 cents per sale of the piece throughout posting. Payments will be made quarterly on or before April 30, July 31, October 30, and January 31.

New Concept Publishing
www.newconceptspublishing.com

Royalties: One dollar for each disk or download sold directly through the site.

NiteLinks
www.nitelinks.com

Royalties: Remuneration is a sliding-scale royalty of 10% to 40% based on gross sales.

Online Originals
http://www.onlineoriginals.com

Royalties: 50% royalty on all titles they sell.

Superior Books
http://www.superiorbooks.com

Royalties: 50% of the selling price, less any tax on the sale. The author's percentage on soft and hard covers will also be 50% but will be based on gross profit, less taxes at point of sale. In addition, if another publisher purchases your work, you will be entitled to 80% of advances and royalties, and SuperiorBooks.com, Inc. will receive a 20% commission.

Virtual Book.com

www.virtualbookworm.com

Royalties: 50% on a 'ready to go' e-book. Other royalties vary depending on choice of 'package'.

Wordbeams.com

www.wordbeams.com

Royalties: 35% of the U.S. retail download price.

World Wrangler Publishing Inc

www.worldwrangler.com

Royalties: 50% of the retail price (attached file, diskette, CD) in US Dollars (USD) on all sales as long as they are sold through WWP or a WWP-approved vendor. This does not include discounted sales to the Author. Royalties will be paid quarterly.

Zander ebooks

www.zanderebooks.com

Royalties: 70% royalties on the list price of e-books that are 50,000 words or more in length, and 50% royalties for books with fewer than 50,000 words. Payments are made on a quarterly basis.

Zeus Publications

http://www.zeus-publications.com

Royalties: 30% on all retail sales.

1st Books

http://www.1stlibrary.com/

Royalties: 100% for first $300, 40% thereafter, 30% on print version.

3

OTHER INFORMATION

Copyright

What is copyright? Briefly it is 'the legal exclusive right of the author of a creative work to control the copying of that work'. Copyright is not a monopoly right, it is simply a right to stop anyone copying your material. Under UK law, material on the internet is protected by copyright and the representation of creativity in which copyright subsists are: original literary, dramatic, musical and artistic works, sound recordings, films, broadcasts and cable programmes.

The availability of material on the internet and the 'free for all' nature of the technology can lead to a relaxed attitude towards copyright laws. The internet has been characterised as the biggest threat to copyright since its creation. It is worth remembering that although everything you create belongs to you, it makes sense to place copyright notices on text documents by adding your name and date, and the copyright symbol ©. In reality, everything on the internet is protected by copyright law, but you must remember that the definition of a creative work is that it exists in some tangible form; it cannot just be a thought, you must have put it in writing. There is no copyright on ideas. Under the Berne Convention, which all major nations have signed, every creative work is copyrighted the moment it is fixed in a tangible from and the internet is no exception to this.

The problem with copyright on the internet lies in enforcement; the internet is so huge and so truly international that you probably won't ever know if someone has infringed your copyright. It can help to make a clear statement setting out the extent to which you are happy for others to use your material without permission.

If you have any concerns that your copyright is being infringed or you want to look into the matter in more detail, visit these sites:

OTHER INFORMATION

Authors Licensing & Copyright Society
www.alcs.co.uk

The Society of Authors
www.writersorg.co.uk

The Copyright Site
www.benedict.com

Contract

Most e-publishers provide a copy of their contract on site (if they don't ask them to supply one). However, this doesn't count for much if you don't understand the elements within a contract. Most e-book publishing contracts seem to be reasonably fair. Generally, there are no costs to the author, although there are many exceptions to this rule. Royalty rates range from 25-70%, paid quarterly in most instances and they usually ask for electronic rights for a specific term. All of these, however, vary from site to site and one must consider all the key points. Remember that although email agreements are binding, it is better to use a contract.

Royalty Rates

Royalties are simply an agreed percentage paid to the author on the sale of each e-book. So if your e-book is priced at £3.50 and the royalty rate is 50% you will get £1.75 for each e-book sold and the e-publisher will get £1.75 on each sale. So you need to find out what a particular e-publisher's royalty rate is. It should be somewhere between 20-50%. Royalties are generally paid at regular intervals, normally quarterly. All of these points should be clearly stated in the contract. There is an argument which suggests that royalty rates should be much higher on the internet when one considers how little work some e-publishers put into producing and promoting works and a standard rate of 50% seems the likely outcome.

Grant of rights

Electronic rights give the e-publisher the right to publish your e-book in electronic form. If they ask for all rights then you will not be allowed to publish the work elsewhere, including in print. If they ask for print rights find out if they are going to publish the manuscript. Most e-publishers ask for electronic rights alone, leaving you free to pursue a print-based publisher. Be very careful that you know exactly what rights the contract stipulates.

Contract Period

The contract period signifies how long the contract will be binding once you have signed it. Find out how long the contract period lasts, when it starts and when it ends. Will they allow you to end the contract by giving a period of notice or do you have to see the contract out? Will they release you immediately if you find a print-publisher?

Costs

The contract should clearly state what fees are involved. Most e-publishers don't charge anything for e-publishing a book, some charge for cover art or formatting material, others charge for editing. Find out what expenses you may have to pay and if there are any hidden charges. Do you have to pay for promotion, for instance?

Copyright

Authors should retain the copyright of their work on the internet just as they do in print.

OTHER INFORMATION

Creative Control

If the e-publisher you are interested in undertakes no editorial work, the author should retain creative control by default. This means you must have the final say on the content of your work.

Termination

Every contract should have a termination clause that protects both the publisher and the author. This means if the publisher does not pay your royalties on time or at all you can terminate the contract at short notice. If you do not keep your side of the bargain then the publisher has equal rights to terminate the contract.

E-publishing contracts should state the above categories as an absolute minimum, but you may find that they will also include sections on **Sales, Promotion, and Format.**

These elements are equally as important; you will need to know how your chosen e-publisher is planning to sell your e-book, promote it and what formats it is likely to be available in. However, an author should take nothing for granted and must become actively involved in the promotion and marketing of their e-book; some e-publishers insist on it as part of the contract.

Sample contract

The Author Network - Contract
www.author.network.com

Author Network publishing agreement between.........................and the Author Network partners.

Agreement made on.......................2000 between.................Author and Author Network partners.

Agreements

1. Definitions and Interpretation

Author is the person holding copyright and full title in the Manuscript

Author Network is the partnership trading as author-network.com from...

Agreed Sum is the amount calculated in Schedule 1

Manuscript means a literary, musical and artistic work listed in Schedule 1 and includes any editions of them and any part or parts of the manuscript that is printed, reprinted, revised or new editions of the manuscript.

Author Network website means the location on the World Wide Web known as author-network.com

Internet Right means the exclusive right to market and sell the Manuscript in electronic form using the World Wide Web or any other digital format including translation but not to reproduce the Manuscript in the form of a film or video or except for Subsidiary Rights to make further uses of the Manuscript without the prior approval of the Author.

Internet Transcription means the format in which the Manuscript is prepared by Author Network for Internet usage.

A reference to this Agreement includes any recitals of and schedules to this agreement including this agreement when amended with the written agreement of both parties to this agreement.

2. Grant of Rights

The Author grants the Internet Right and the Subsidiary Uses to Author Network.

3. Author Obligations

3.1 The Author shall deliver manuscripts to Author Network in an agreed format, that is as electronic text in MS Word or RTF format capable of being read by a PC platform computer.

4. Author Network Obligations

Prepare the Author's manuscript for electronic publication in such format(s) as Author Network considers necessary.

Ensure a copyright notice is included when the manuscript is displayed on the screen acknowledging the Author.

Encrypt the manuscript to impede unauthorised electronic copying.

Promote and market the Manuscript as Author Network think fit.

5. Payment to Author

Author Network must pay the Agreed Sum to the Author

Author Network will provide the Author with a statement relating to Author Network services every three months and pay the Agreed Sum within 30 days of the balance date.

6. Internet Transcription

Author Network owns the copyright in the Internet Transcription while the Author retains copyright to the Manuscript.

7. Warranties

The Author warrants that:

They control the Internet Rights to the work and that the rights do not infringe the intellectual property rights of any person or create any legally enforceable claim by any other party other than the parties to this agreement.

No proceedings have been instituted by any third party for the title or any infringement of intellectual property rights in the books.

No material in the manuscript is defamatory or will infringe the rights of any person in any country.

The Author has not entered into any agreements that are inconsistent with this agreement.

The Author Network warrants that:

The Author Network will meet the reasonable expectations of customers as to quality and service.

The Internet Transcription will be made available to the Author prior to publication

Every effort will be made to ensure that manuscript is properly prepared for publication, taking heed of all information supplied by the Author.

SCHEDULE 1

The Manuscript with the Title.....................................The right to which is held by ....to be identified as the Author as asserted in accordance with the Copyright, Designs and Patents Act 1988 is to be published in electronic format suitable for sale by electronic transfer by Author Network.

The Author Network will pay the Author,..................................., the Agreed Sum being a percentage of 45% of the selling price of the Internet Transcription for sales made from the Author Network website.

The Author Network will take 10% of the final selling price of the Subsidiary Rights it obtains from any agreements made in respect of the Internet Transcription with any third party.

For the avoidance of doubt the Author retains the right to publish the manuscript in book form, video or film, giving the Author Network partners first right of refusal to act as the Author's agent in such circumstances for a percentage, to be negotiated, of the final selling price of any of these rights."

Signed............................. Author

Signed............................. Author-network.com

OTHER INFORMATION

E-book Rights

E-book rights are a complicated issue. But it is important that authors get to grips with the subject and understand the issues involved. Much of the discussion at the moment involves the link between electronic rights and royalties and why they should be negotiated separately. Royalties for e-books are much higher than for print books, and therefore you will need to clarify the distinction bearing in mind the industry standard for e-books seems set to peak at 50%, against an average 10% for print books. If you sign over your electronic rights to your publisher under a normal print contract not only will you be giving away electronic royalties, at the same rate as print royalties, you will no longer be free to publish the material anywhere else. It is strongly recommended that you negotiate electronic rights and royalties, accordingly, as a separate issue to other rights.

There has been much discussion between the Publishers Association, The Society of Authors, and the Association of Authors Agents in an attempt to clarify the position for all those concerned and to reach some consensus on electronic rights in the UK. The Publishers Association released a background paper late in 2000, entitled, 'Electronic Verbatim Text Rights' and stated that 'Volume rights author/grantor contracts include all verbatim text rights exclusively for all media, except where specifically excluded, for the territory covered by the contracts concerned.' Both the Society of Authors and the Association of Authors Agents failed to agree to this. The Publishers Association then stated that 'many publishers would explicitly seek electronic verbatim text rights' meaning they would assume that electronic rights comes with the territory. However, they also suggested publishers clarify that they are also acquiring electronic rights specifically.

The trend appears to be that an author will be asked for electronic rights with the issue of a new contract. The Society of Authors recommends that authors should retain all electronic rights, but they also need to know how to negotiate these rights in a controlled way. Visit the Society of Authors website for more information, www.writers.org.uk/society, or email them at authorsoc@writers.org.uk. Or visit The Publishers Association at www.publishers.org.uk or email them at mail@publishers.org.uk. The Associations of Authors' Agents can be contacted on 020 7387 2076.

Search Methods

- *Latest estimate of web pages on the World Wide Web: 1 to 2.1 billion*
- *People who spend five or more hours a week online spend 71% of their time searching for information.*
- *85-90% of all Internet users rely on search engines to locate sites.*
- *93% of Internet users never look past the first three pages of search results.*

We all know search engines and directories exist but what we *really* need to know is how to use them to good effect and considering the statistics above, it seems even more essential. Search engines and directories can be classified into general categories depending on the material or information you are searching for. I have put together a list of the most successful internet search engines and to help you tailor a search to suit your specific needs I have provided an overview of how to use each search engine and directory listed.

There is a slight distinction between search engines and directories. **AltaVista** for example, is a search engine. Search engines use specialised software to scan the internet, often referred to as robots, spiders and crawlers. They look for information on web pages and store the information in enormous databases specific to that search engine. **Yahoo**, however, is a directory. Web directories use humans to find and organise material. Directories structure their information differently. Yahoo, for instance, makes information available through a list of 14 top-level categories. However, the distinction between Web directories and search engines is becoming less obvious. Yahoo, one of the first directories on the Web, offers the option of searching by keyword. Web search engines like **Lycos** and **Infoseek** give users the choice to browse links by subject. Excite offers topical searches and links to "related" pages with their search results.

The key thing to remember is that search engines are only as effective as the terms you supply. If you don't include as many phrases or words as you should, or you misspell words, or you are searching for the wrong thing, the results will be flawed.

To begin with it may help to limit yourself to the major search engines and progress from there. Always use a search engine's 'advanced search' help facility, these will give you detailed instructions on the best way to conduct a search according to their requirements and will give you the best chance of securing the information you are looking for. Obviously one search engine can't find everything on the Web. The amount of information available on the internet grows every minute as new pages are listed and old ones are replaced, expanded or removed.

Useful tips

- **Create a list of keywords**

Create a list of keywords and phrases before you use the search engines. Your list should be designed to produce the longest list of relevant pages from the search engines. Enter the words or phrases into a few selected search engines. When you see the results of your searches, add new terms from the results to your own list of keywords.

- **Define your search**

Finding results with a search engine is not a problem; the challenge is to create a search that excludes irrelevant pages. To search for documents or pages about writing articles, start by entering the keywords **"writing"** or **"articles"** to see what comes up. If you look at the results you might find that the words **"writing"** and **"articles"** will appear separately in many documents. If you enter the word **"freelance"** you might find that **"freelance"** will appear separately in many documents too. You need some way to link these words so that the pages include combinations of these words to get the best results. To do this you need to use operators.

- **Learn to use "operators"**

Operators are symbols or special words that sit alongside the keywords in a query and tell the search engine how to process them. These can be used to refine searches. Operators let users specify whole phrases or words to exclude, or words that should appear, and words that should appear close together.

Phrase searching

With AltaVista, Infoseek, Excite, and Yahoo!, it is possible to specify phrases by putting them in quotation marks (""). It should have become clear that if you put the keywords **writing** or **articles** into a search engine it produces too many irrelevant hits. You are not looking for all of the documents that contain the keywords **writing** and **articles** or even **freelance** you are trying to find only those documents that contain the phrase **"writing articles"** and/or the word **freelance.**

Try searching for the whole phrase **"writing articles"** and compare the results with the **writing** and **articles** search.

Includes and Excludes (+/-)

To make the search even more precise, you can include and exclude certain terms. If you add a plus sign (+) in front of a term in the search box, the search engine will know that the term must appear in the pages. If you add a minus sign (-) in front of a term, the search engine knows that the term must not appear in the pages.

Boolean logic (AND, OR, NOT, NEAR)

AltaVista and Excite use Boolean, or proximity, operators (always in uppercase) instead of includes and excludes (+/-). Boolean operators can add even more specificity to a search. By placing one of the Boolean operators between terms you can include and exclude terms, find cases where terms occur close together, and account for synonyms for words in a phrase. Here are some basic Boolean operators:

Examples:

AND: **writing AND articles:** Find all pages containing both the terms **writing** and **articles** anywhere on the page.

OR: **writing OR articles OR freelance:** Find all pages containing the term **writing.** Find all the pages containing the term **articles.** And all pages containing the term **freelance.**

AND NOT: **writing AND NOT fiction:** Find all pages that contain the term **fiction.** Of those pages, exclude ones that contain the term **fiction.**

NEAR: **writing NEAR articles:** Find all pages that contain the terms **writing** and **articles** within 10 spaces of each other.

Several operators can be used at once with parentheses to create even more complex searches. But be careful where you put the parentheses:

Examples:

(writing OR articles) AND freelance: Find pages that contain the terms **writing** and **articles.** Find pages that contain **articles** and **freelance.**

writing OR (articles AND freelance): Find pages that contain the term **writing.** Find pages that contain the terms **articles** and **freelance.**

(writing NEAR articles) AND freelance: Find pages that contain the phrase **writing** within 10 characters of the term **articles** and contain the term **freelance** somewhere on the page.

Search engines

AOL
http://search.aol.com

AOL is now using Inktomi for search results and the Open Directory project for directory results. AOL formerly used a co-branded version of Excite in North America. While in Europe, AOL used a version of Lycos for results.

Search Tips:
Near the bottom of your AOL Search results page you will probably find a list of related searches. For example, if you searched on the single word **baseball**, you might see the following: People who searched for **baseball** also searched for:
Baseball Hall of Fame | Major League Baseball | fantasy baseball | college baseball | NCAA baseball | baseball
    One word searches often yield too many results. Instead, type in multiple words or a phrase in quotes to give the system a better idea of what you want. For example, to find information on the Better Business Bureau, type in **"Better Business Bureau"** (in quotes). This tells AOL Search to retrieve only those documents that contain that exact phrase. If you don't use quotes, AOL Search still looks for documents containing all of those words, but documents containing the exact phrase might end up further down the list.

AltaVista
http://www.altavista.com

Alta Vista went online in 1995. It started in DEC's research lab in Palo Alto, CA. AltaVista inventions have included the first-ever multi-lingual search capability on the internet and the first search technology to support Chinese, Japanese and Korean languages via its translator Babel Fish. It was the web's first internet machine translation service that can translate words, phrases or entire web sites in English to and from Spanish, French, German, Portuguese, Italian and Russian. Alta also has a multimedia search to explore the web for photos, videos and music, with an estimated index of over 90 million multimedia objects.

Alta Vista recently added Ask Jeeves search technology in 1999 (you can now put questions to AltaVista instead of just keywords).

Search Tips:

You can search the AltaVista index by typing words, phrases, or questions in the search box. The search automatically sorts the results so the most relevant Web pages are listed first.

Type words related to the information you are looking for. Type your inquiry in the form of a question, a statement, or a phrase. Or you can just list a few words (keywords) related to what you are trying to find. You can include quotation marks to delineate a phrase, and plus or minus signs to require or exclude words.

*AskJeeves

http://askjeeves.com

Enter your question, in plain English, in the text box on the Ask Jeeves front page (the first page you see after you type in **www.ask.com**), then click on the **"ASK"** button (you may also press the **"Enter"** key on your keyboard, depending on which browser you're using). It will respond by presenting you with one or more closely related questions to which AskJeeves knows the answer.

Certain AskJeeves questions contain lists from which you can select an item by clicking on the text box that is part of the question. To answer some questions, it will ask you a follow-up question; think of this as "clarification", to give you the best possible answer. Once you've chosen the AskJeeves question that best fits the question you entered, click on the **"ASK!"** button and it will take you to an internet site that answers your question.

DogPile

http://dogpile.com

Has an online Custom Search form. Here are the details:

Using their form you can set the order that the DogPile Meta-Search Engine will use to send your query to 14 search engines that they metasearch.

Choose which search engine you would like to be first, second, and so on. If you do not want a particular engine to be included in your custom search, choose "—skip—". Do not worry about blank spots or duplicates. They will automatically be removed. Note that your browser must be cookie-capable (Netscape or MSIE version 2 or better). When you are done, press the **"Save new search order"** button.

Excite

http://www.excite.com and www.excite.co.uk

Excite went online in December 1995. In mid 1996, Excite acquired Magellan and later in 1996 also purchased WebCrawler. Excite also includes its directory service, Excite Channels.

Users may also search specific news stories. However, these news stories are not archived and fall off the system within a few weeks. It offers both keyword-based searching and concept-based searching (it will not only search for the terms you type in but also similar terms). Excite lost its spot as the search engine of choice on AOL Netfind and on Netscape in 1999. As of July 2000 it is using Looksmart for directory services.

Search Tips:

Excite provides an online power search form which is really handy. But they provide a list of 'General Search Tips': Search for ideas and concepts instead of just keywords by using more than one word in your search. Excite's search results are sorted by relevance. The results nearest the top will usually be the most relevant. Use more descriptive, specific words as opposed to general ones. Try an Advanced Search. Use the **+(plus)** sign for words that your results MUST contain. Or use the - (**minus**) sign in your query to tell the search engine that your results should NOT contain a certain word. When using these options, do not leave any space between the sign and the word.

Fast/AllTheWeb
http://ussc.alltheweb.com

Fast or AllTheWeb.com is owned and operated by Fast Search & Transfer ASA technologies. It went online in 1998 with one of the largest databases available at the time. One of their strengths has been the development of Multimedia specific search engines. They also have one of the largest databases of FTP URLs for mp3, wav, ra, and other multimedia file types. They feed not only FTP search results but also web page results to Lycos. The company was originally called Fast Internet Transfer. FAST is an acronym for Fast Search & Transfer. Search & Transfer ASA (FAST) was formally established in Oslo, Norway, on July 16, 1997.

Fast is also noted as the only major search engine to currently embrace PHP technology on its home page - and has the best looking homepage of all search engine companies.

Search Tips:
A Simple Search is done by filling in a search query in the text box and press the **"FAST Search"** button. A search query is generally a combination of words, but you can also use the following special characters to further refine the search: **+word:** all search results will contain this word. Equates to a Boolean **AND**. -**word:** the search results will not contain this word. Equates to a Boolean **NOT**. **"word1 word2":** You can group several words by putting quotes around them, defining a phrase (**word1 word2**): The search results will contain one or more of the words. Equates to a Boolean **OR**. Note: Only one level of parenthesis may be used

Go.com

http://www.go.com

Here's a quick overview of how to search Go.com.

1. In the Search box, type one or more phrases that describe what you're looking for, like good minestrone soup recipe. If you want to search for two proper names, separate them with a comma, like this: **Bill Gates, Microsoft.**

2. Choose where you want to search from the list near the Search box.

The choices are:

- The Web: a comprehensive index of Web sites.
- Topics: a handpicked directory of quality Web sites.
- News: a collection of recent news stories.
- Companies: brief company biographies.
- Newsgroups: messages in Usenet discussion areas.

3. Click the Find button.

A new page appears in your Web browser listing the first page of search results. Click a result to view it. For more information, see Viewing search results. If you don't like the results and you want to improve them, see refining your search.

*Google

http://www.google.com

Google has been online since late 1997. They recently added its page rank algorithm to a branded edition of the Open Directory Project. On July 1, they announced that they would become the provider of search results for non-directory matches on Yahoo. In mid 1999 it received $20 million dollars investment.

Google offers some of the most unique results of any search engine. Using a system called PageRank, Google filters a large portion of irrelevant results. It also has a built in bias towards EDU and GOV sites that makes a change from the other .com spam infested search engines. Google currently lists 25 million pages in its database, and is getting set for a major crawl to put in over 100 million pages. On June 3, 1999 Google received an influx of capital ($25 million) from

Sequoia Capital. In mid 2000 they were chosen as the premier provider of search results on Yahoo.

Search Tips:
Has an advanced online search form to fill in as well as offering specialised search forms for specific topics.

GoTo.com
http://www.goto.com

Idealab founded GoTom, and was the first major search engine to successfully auction search results. Its arrival on the internet prompted some hostile reactions, but it has earned a strong reputation with webmasters based upon quality business dealings. GoTo has been rock solid in its customer relations over the years and makes no apologies for selling results.

GoTo uses Inktomi for non-paid search results, but only lists the first 15 hits. One of the lowest bandwidth (fast loading) search engines on the net. Purchased the World Wide Web Worm in early 1998, developed by Oliver McBryan in 1994, which was one of the first robot-driven search engines. GoTo's value as a legitimate search engine is still in doubt and its sales of key words is questionable.

Search Tips:
All you have to do is type in a keyword or click on one of their keyword links and you'll be instantly taken to a list of results.

You may also type the keyword(s) (like **"Sporting Goods"**), that describe what you're looking for, into the search box that is on the GoTo home page. Search boxes are also located at the top and bottom of every results page. After you type in your keyword(s), hit the green **"find it"** or arrow button and you'll be taken immediately to the results you're looking for.

HotBot/Lycos (now one and the same see Lycos)
http://www.lycos.hotbot.com

Hotbot went online in May 1996. Search results are served by the Inktomi database. It formerly used LookSmart for categorised directory of site listings but switched to The Open Directory Project in mid 1999. Paul Gauthier and Eric Brewer originally created Inktomi, at the University of California, Berkeley. Hotbot also uses the Direct Hit click through data to manipulate results.

Search Tips:
They have an extensive advanced search online form.

Infoseek/Go.com
http://www.infoseek.com/ or www.go.com

Infoseek went online in August 1995 as a directory service. Infoseek is now part of the Disney GO network having sold a full percentage stake to Disney.

After toying with the whole site directory model, Infoseek still spiders occasionally. It also is building a large directory of sites cross-linked to search results (GoDirectory).

LookSmart
http://www.looksmart.com/

LookSmart went online in October 1996. It currently lists over 600,000 sites in its directory database. LookSmart provides categorised directory listings for AltaVista, HotBot and over 1000 Internet access sellers (ISP's). Reader's Digest funded LookSmart until late 1997 when a group of company investors bought out the RD shares.

Search Tips:
Keyword Search quickly finds specific names, titles and terms within the

LookSmart directory and throughout the millions of sites in the AltaVista index. Just type a word or phrase into the bar in the yellow search panel and click on Search.

Keyword Search Tip: Think big! Don't worry if you end up with a large number of results, because the most relevant content will always be listed first. If you find that your search results are too broad, then go back and add some more specific terms. Remember that you'll get more precise results by typing **"chocolate chip cookie recipe"** than, for example, just **"cookie"** in the search box.

You can search three ways with the tools at LookSmart: Category Search, Keyword Search and LookSmart Live!

Lycos
http://www.lycos.com/

Lycos was developed from a research project at Carnegie Mellon University by Dr. Michael Mauldin and went online in 1994. The name Lycos comes from the Latin for "wolf spider." Standard search results via Lycos Pro, and categorised listings via WiseWire.

Lycos then purchased Wired Digital - acquiring HotBot search engine in the process and it has added the ODP directory to its line-up. The Lycos Network now consists of: Gamesville, Tripod, WhoWhere, Lycos Communications, Angelfire, Hotbot, Hotwired, Wired News, Quote, Sonique, and Webmonkey.

Search Tips:

Lycos keeps track of every word on each page in the freshest catalogue on the Web. That's a lot of information, so you can improve your search results by being specific. For example, if you're thinking of buying a new computer and looking for suggestions, you'll get more than you bargained for if you simply type the word **"computer"** into the search box and click the **"Find"** button. Instead, you'll be shopping sooner if you phrase your search like this: Search for: **computer-buying guide** When searching, consider what words you might use to describe a subject if you were a webmaster.

To learn how to supercharge your searches with the Search Options and the Power Panel, see their Search Options help section.

Netscape
http://www.netscape.com/

Netscape Netcenter is a major focal point for search engine traffic. In 1998, Netscape released the 4.06 version of its browser with keyword searching direct from the location address. Search results are currently fed by Excite with other search engines filling out a "featured engine" list.

Search Tips:
To perform a search, simply enter the terms you are searching for and click on the "Search" button. Searches with multiple terms will automatically insert an **"and"** between all the terms, so that only sites with all of the search words in them will be returned. For example, a search on **golf clubs** will return sites that have both **golf and clubs** in the site's name and description. Sites on **"tennis clubs"** or **"golf balls"** will not be displayed (unless they also mention golf and clubs). If no sites are found that contain both terms, sites that contain either term will be displayed.

Nktomi
http://www.inktomi.com/

Inktomi was founded in 1996 by two researchers at Berkeley, University of California, Eric Brewer and Paul Gauthier. The company's name, pronounced "INK-tuh-me," is derived from a Lakota Indian legend about a trickster spider character. Inktomi is known for his ability to defeat larger adversaries through wit and cunning.

Past and present Inktomi partners include: HotBot, AOL Netfind, Yahoo, ICQ, iWon, GeoCities, Search MSN, GoTo, Snap, Aeneid, N2H2, Anzwers.au, Goo.jp, Canada.com, RadarUol, ICQit.com Yahoo, and Searchopolis.

Not only is Inktomi a powerful search engine, it is also a master in the powerful technology of directory building via spidered page results. Their directory engine uses a technology called "Concept Induction" which automatically analyses and categorises millions of documents. Concept Induction incorporates algorithms that model human conceptual understanding of information.

Northern Light
http://www.northernlight.com

Northern Light started in 1995 in the basement of an old mill building in Cambridge, Massachusetts and went online in 1997. It currently has one of the largest databases in its directory courtesy of its crawler Gulliver. However, it has never produced users and is ignored by webmasters as a source of referrals.

At the end of 1998, they had added precision search enhancements, advanced search forms, real-time news, thousands of Special Collection publications, and millions of web pages. Today they have nearly 200 employees.

Search Tips:
To increase the precision of your search results, Northern Light requires most of the words in your search to be present in the result documents. To gain more control over your results, they provide the following hints:

Northern Light supports natural language searching. To find information on your topic of interest, try typing a question into the search bar. Example: **What is the capital of Sweden?**

You can also search with simple words. The more words you enter, the more on-target your results will be. Examples: **ski resorts Vermont (instead of skiing) ergonomic workstation mouse keyboard (instead of ergonomics).**

Northern Light supports full Boolean capability **(AND, OR, NOT)**, including parenthetical expressions, in all search forms. Supports the use of double quotes around specific phrases and the **+(plus)** and **-(minus)** signs to include and exclude words.

Search.com
http://www.search.com/

Yet another of Cnet's sites. This one has search results fed by Infoseek. There is also a small set of listings built by its own in-house crawling left over from when they first went online.

Search Tips:

If you're looking for general information and resources, the best place to start is the main search box at http://www.search.com/. Just enter your query (**e.g. pokemon**) and press the Search button. Your results will include links to relevant categories in Web directories (like Yahoo! or About) as well as to Web pages, headlines, and prices on related products.

Specific categories
Choose a metasearch channel from their main page. Each of the channels searches specialised engines related to that particular topic or genre. For example, the Music channel gives you the option to search for MP3's, lyrics, reviews, prices, software, concert tickets and more. You can select as many categories as you like on a particular channel. The more checkboxes you select, the more engines they search.

Snap/NBCi
http://www.snap.com/ or www.nbci.com

Snap is another Cnet site, now owned and operated by NBCi. Snap is set-up in the directory fashion of Yahoo or Looksmart. When a search fails, results are fed by Inktomi. Snap also has partnerships with Microsoft and NBC.

The ODP is a web site directory built by volunteers. The database now holds approximately 1,200,000 sites (3-3-2000). Netscape, Lycos, Hotbot, AltaVista, AOL Netfind, Google, and a host of smaller sites use the ODP.

Search Tips:
If you have a general subject in mind (like **"baseball"),** type the word or words in

248

the Search box and click the Search button. NBCi will search its entire collection of hand-picked sites for those that contain words from your query. The more matches NBCi finds for a website, the more prominently it will be featured in your search results. If no matching sites are found, NBCi automatically searches the rest of the Web for results.

If you know exactly what you want, you can get better results by entering very specific information into the Search box. NBCi allows you to use three methods to refine your search: searching for an exact phrase enter quotes (" ") around terms to require that the entire phrase be found in the search. For example, **"royals baseball"** returns listings where the words **"royals"** and **"baseball"** appear together and in that order, either in the title, the URL of the Web site or the document.

Supports the **+(plus)** and **-(minus)** signs to include and exclude words.

UK Plus
http://www.ukplus.co.uk

Type one or more words ("keywords") into the search box, describing the type of sites you want to find on the internet ("I want to know about") and click the Search button.

For example, if you want a hotel somewhere in the Lake District, and want to book a room over the Internet, you could type in: hotel Lake District booking reservation. Don't forget to put spaces between each of the words, and use no punctuation. This will bring up a choice of web sites for suitable hotels. If you know the precise name of the town you'd like to stay in, type that instead of "Lake District". The Search Results may include lots of other hotels to help you too, but those closest to your search criteria will be at the top of the page. Remember, the more precise you are with your search, the more accurate the response you'll get from UK Plus.

Advanced Search Techniques
UK Plus supports the use of **+(plus)** and **-(minus)** signs to include and exclude words.

Use Brackets

Brackets group portions of more complicated queries together. Depending on whether

Manchester or university is the more important for your search, your university search may look like this: **(universities OR colleges)+manchester.**

WebCrawler

http://www.webcrawler.com/

WebCrawler went online in 1994, and is another search engine that started out life as research project - this one at the University of Washington, by Brian Pinkerton. AOL bought it in 1995 and it was then bought by Excite in late 1996. Although owned by Excite, it still runs WebCrawler as a stand alone search engine. Webcrawler is noted as the first major search engine to author and use the Robots Exclusion Standard and it supports "natural language searching"

Search Tips:

WebCrawler supports **"natural language searching"** so that users can type their searches in plain English without worrying about mastering complex search syntax. Although if you do happen to be a master of complex search syntax, you'll be happy to know that WebCrawler also supports a wide range of Boolean search operators. See ***Advanced Searching for details***

WebCrawler matches any or all of your search terms

To use WebCrawler's Search Feature, you just need to be able to describe what you're looking for with a series of words or a phrase, and then click the **"Search"** button. When you type in a series of search terms, WebCrawler is programmed to find results that match any or all of those words. However, WebCrawler assumes that you're most interested in results that contain all of the words you entered and gives those documents a higher relevance score so they appear at the top of the list. Because the default search method is to find any or all of the terms, WebCrawler also returns pointers to pages that contain some of the words.

For example, the search **NASA space shuttle program** will produce pointers near the top of the results list that contain all of those words but will also include results that contain references only to **NASA** or **space** or **shuttle** or **program.**

Yahoo! http://www.yahoo.com or www.uk.yahoo.com

Yahoo went online in August of 1994 and is currently one of the oldest directory services on the net. Founded by David Filo and Jerry Yang, Ph.D. candidates in Electrical Engineering at Stanford University. They started their guide in April 1994 as a way to keep track of their own personal interests on the internet.

The name Yahoo is alleged to stand for "Yet Another Hierarchical Officious Oracle," but Filo and Yang say they selected the name because they considered themselves yahoos.

Yahoo used to be a sentimental favourite of everyone on the internet, however that has changed a great deal in the last year. Webmasters have become increasingly frustrated with the low rate of submitted sites entering the database, which stands at about 4%. Yahoo has been adding alternative options (chat, message boards, free email, home pages, yahoo clubs) to its site over the last year to try and regain lost ground.

Search Tips:

Specify a keyword or set of keywords, and Yahoo will search its entire database to find listings that match the keywords you provide.

After you have specified keyword(s) inside the query box and clicked on the search button, Yahoo will search through the five areas of its database for keyword matches.

The first page returned to you will be a list of matching Yahoo Categories followed by a list of matching Yahoo Sites. If no matching Yahoo Categories and Sites are found, Yahoo will automatically perform a Web-wide, full-text document search using the Google search engine.

You are able to access a list of matching News Articles and Net Events by clicking on the links in the menu bar at the top of the pages.

If you want to further customise your search, you have two options at your disposal:

1. Go to the search options page and follow the instructions, or

2. Specify options along with the keywords inside the query box using their advanced search syntax.

It is helpful to use more than search engine at a time, or all of them. You will find that you get different results from each one. Not all websites are registered with all search engines and not all of the results you are given will be relevant. When a website is submitted to a search engine the use of keywords will only reflect some of the web content. This can mean that you may have to visit each website to find out if the material on the site is relevant, which can be very time consuming. Specialist search engines are also available:

The BBC Webguide
http://www.bbc.co.uk/education/webguide/

Beaucoup
http://www.beaucoup.com

A good place to learn about your subject can be from newspapers, magazines and trade periodicals, many of which have an online presence.

The Internet Public Library
www.ipl.org/

The Electronic News Stand
http://www.enews.com

Contact other online authors and publishers using email lists, forums and news-groups to ask questions specific to your topic.

A comprehensive list of forums and mailing lists can be found at:

Forum One
http://www.forumone.com

Another site for mailing lists, forums and newsgroups is **Liszt**, the mailing list directory at: http://www.liszt.com. Or look for ezines at **eZine Search**: http://ezinesearch.com.

NB. Search engines and directories are subject to frequent take-overs and restructuring.

Resources for Freelance Writers

The best advice for would be freelance writers can often be found by reading online articles by published authors. Many of the sites listed offer advice to writers of all genres.

Burning Void Writers' Resources Page

www.burningvoid.com/users/heather/writing/resources.html

Good selection of articles on some tricky issues such as 'Pay per click sites & the professional writer'.

For Writers Only

www.forwriters.com

Author websites, markets, writers groups and reference sites.

Freelance Journal

www.home/eunet.no/~trondhu/

Lots of articles on writing non-fiction and photojournalism.

Freelance Writers

http://freelancewrite.about.com/careers/freelancewrite/

Offers a multitude of articles, guides and tips for writers by professional freelance writers. Good for beginners.

PageOne

www.pageonelit.com

Literary Newsletter and website of resources for writers. Interviews and writing tips.

Readers' & Writers' Resources

www.diane.com/readers/

Many articles on journalism, technical writing and freelancing.

Shaw Guides

http://writing.shawguides.com

Provides many links to international conferences, workshops and sites that give inside information and tips of the trade.

Tech Pubs

www.techpubs.com

Resources for technical writing, including professional associations, mailing lists and technical writing design.

The Burry Man Writers Centre

www.burryman.com

Resources for fiction and non-fiction writers, working professionals and beginners with particular support for writing about Scotland.

The Eclectic Writer

www.eclectics.com/writing/writing.html

Offers a good selection of articles advising writers on subjects such as manuscript format, electronic publishing and writing a synopsis. A brilliant Character Chart for fiction writers and online discussion board.

The European Journalism Page

www.demon.co.uk/eurojournalism/general.html

Sites and resources of interest to journalists writing in or covering Europe.

The Online Communicator

www.communicator.com

Articles on writing for all types of media on the internet.

The Reporters Network

www.reporters.net

The Reporters Network was formed in October 1995 by Bob Sablatura, a reporter for the Houston Chronicle, to promote the Internet as a research and communications medium for working journalists.

The Web Writer

www.geocities.com/Athens/Parthenon/8390/TOC.htm

This site provides a broad range of information from getting online to building a web site, but is basically a site for writers who want to publish material on the internet.

Write News

www.writenews.com

An extensive news media database with over 1000 links. Free newsletter.

WriteRead.com

http://www.writeread.com

A major new portal for writers. Offering articles, books, software, courses, market connections, publishing and other resources, WriteRead promises to bring writers the resources they need to be more successful in their work.

Writers on the Net

www.writers.com

Online writing classes, tutors, and writers' groups. Run by a group of published authors and experienced teachers.

Writers' Resource Center

www.poewar.com/

Freelance job forum, articles and employment centre.

Writers' Toolbox

www.writerstoolbox.com

Diverse collection of online resources for writers.

Writers' Website

www.writerswebsite.com

Many links to useful resources by category.

OTHER INFORMATION

Competitions

Winning a competition can increase a writer's confidence, may lead to publication, and provides the occasional monetary compensation. Entering competitions on the internet is as easy as submitting material to an ezine; they usually post guidelines and submission procedures clearly on the site, with details of themes, length and in what format to submit the material.

A plan of attack:

- ### *Spread out your submissions evenly throughout the year.*
It helps to enter competitions that occur throughout the year because it will leave you time in between to write new stories or consider which stories you will enter for the next competition. If you have a list of possible targets you need to make sure you submit the material on time, and preferably long before the submission deadline.

- ### *Try to write new stories and enter them for each competition.*
It makes sense to produce new material, although of course, you can re-enter stories that you have submitted in the past, but producing new material is vital for any writer. Practice makes perfect and authors are no exception to this rule.

- ### *Enter more than one story per competition.*
Entering more than one story for a competition may seem costly but it will obviously increase your chance of success. One story may catch the eye of a judge where the others didn't.

- ### *Try to be innovative in your writing.*
Although you cannot predict what is going to impress a judge, it makes sense to produce original, innovative material, and it is important to take a look at the website or ezine that is running the competition.

- ### *Don't enter the competition at the last minute.*
This may seem irrelevant but it is a well-known fact that the bulk of competition

entries arrive in the last four weeks before deadlines, which means the poor old judges are going to be left with reading the vast majority of manuscripts in very little time. Those that have been entered early will have been carefully read and possibly re-read; the late arrivals can expect a cursory reading and who can blame the judges for that?

- *Follow guidelines and submission procedures.*

It is also important to read the guidelines and submission procedures of each competition; these will be posted on the website or listed in the ezine. They are there for a reason; follow them. If in doubt query the editor.

- *Research the market.*

Get a feel for the sort of fiction or non-fiction that each website or ezine produces by going to the website that produces the ezine and looking at their content. Read the winning entries listed for previous competitions to get an insider view of what caught the judge's eye the last time round.

Art DEADLINES List
http://custwww.xensei.com/adl/

A curious assortment of competitions, contests, calls for entries/papers, grants, scholarships, fellowships, jobs, internships, etc. in the arts or related areas (painting, drawing, animation, poetry, writing, music, multimedia, reporting/journalism, cartooning, dance, photography, video, film, sculpture, etc), some of which have prizes worth thousands of dollars. International in scope - contests and competitions for students are included.

Byline Contest Page
http://www.bylinemag.com/contests.htm
Features a variety of writing contests where you can enter something as simple as a word game or as big as your self-published book.

OTHER INFORMATION

Contests
http://www.authorlink.com/confren.html
This is a huge listing of national contests to enter.

New Century Writer Awards
http://www.newcenturywriter.org/ncwllc.htm
This competition, in its third year, offers cash prizes to short stories, stage plays, screenplays, and novel excerpts.

The Bulwer-Lytton Fiction Contest
http://www.bulwer-lytton.com
For this contest, entrants must compose the opening sentence for the WORST novel possible.

The Frustrated Writers Society
www.writings.freeserve.co.uk/comp.html
The Society runs quarterly Short Story competitions which are open to the public on payment of an entry fee of £3.00. Each quarter there is a prize of £100, a certificate of merit, plus one years free membership to the Society. Members of the public who enter the competitions can join the Society on special terms. Any genres, thriller, crime, romance, historical.

Writer's Digest
http://www.writersdigest.com/catalog/contest_frame.html
Think you are a good writer? Then check out this site where you have a chance of winning a cash prize for your short story. Pay close attention to deadlines for 2001 and don't miss reading the rules and categories section.

Getting On the Web

It may be that the future lies in writer's developing their own websites and selling their own e-books from their sites. This takes us one step further on from a home-page on which you may wish to provide users with information about yourself. If you have a computer, can use a simple text editor or have WordPad, you can create a site and you can put your novel or manuscript on that site and sell it. Anyone contemplating creating their own website should probably be armed with a good guide to creating HTML or designing a website. If you are an absolute beginner try *The Complete Idiot's Guide - Creating a Web Page* by Paul McFedries published by Alpha books, or if you are looking for something more advanced try *Web Design in a Nutshell - A Desktop Quick Reference* by Jennifer Niederst published by O'Reilly. There are many sites on the internet that will help you with HTML and design; take a look at the following:

Cnet Builder.com
www.home.cnet.com
This is a good site for all website designers, from beginner to expert. Lots of tips and how-tos.

Webmonkey
http://hotwired.lycos.com/webmonkey/index.html
Provides a lot of good tutorials on HTML basics but is good for experts too.

HMTL Writers Guild
www.hwg.org
The HTML Writers Guild is the world's largest international organisation of web authors with over 118,000 members in more than 150 nations worldwide. The community provides resources, support, representation, and education for web authors at all skill levels.

There are a number of steps in the process and it goes without saying that creating a website involves a lot of dedication and time. Here are a few of the basics to consider:

- You will need to learn HTML (HyperText Markup Language) if you are going to create your own web pages. Not as scary as it sounds, it is simply a mark-up language, not a programming language, i.e. a collection of letter and word combinations that creates styles such as bold and italic. With it you can format text, create lists and tables, link to other pages, insert images and much more. You can of course use a text editor such as **CuteHTML** (www.globalscape.com) to create the HTML for you, or FrontPage Express the HTML editing programme that comes with Internet Explorer 4.0, as well as Windows 98 . Both have their advantages and disadvantages. Many webmasters prefer to use WordPad to create their HTML because it allows them so much more control.

- You must have a way of allowing users to access your web pages and to do this you need a website. For this, you need a server, which means access to a computer that can literally dish your material out to the internet. These types of servers are called host providers; they are companies that host your material and store that material on their website. You can use your existing Internet provider, find a free hosting service, or a commercial provider. **Yahoo** has an index of free web providers at: http://www.yahoo.com/Business_and_Economy/Companies/Internet _Services/Web_Services/Free_Web_Pages/. You can find a substantial list of commercial providers at: http://thelist.Internet.com. Many host providers will also allow you to buy your own domain name, which is something well worth considering. The downside of using a freespace site is that it will often state this in the URL. Try **Domain Valet** at www.domainvalet.com.

- Once you have signed up with a provider, they will provide you with a directory on the server that you can use to store your Web page files.

- You can now 'upload' or send your files to the directory created for you on the host provider's Web server. (Some Web hosts offer their own file upload services.) To do this you need FTP (File Transfer Protocol) software. There are several you can use: **CuteFTP**, http://www.cuteftp.com, or **WSFTP**, http://www.ipswitch.com, which is available as a free download.

- You will have to tell CuteFTP (preferred choice) where to find your files, this can be done by running the CuteFTP software; the FTP site

Manager dialogue box will appear, highlight Personal FTP Sites, and then select the 'add site' button. The FTP Site Edit box will appear. In the Site Label box enter a name for the site, i.e. My Writing Site, not the URL. In the Host Address box, enter the name of your host provider, i.e. www.yourhost.com. Your host provider may give you an FTP address, in which case enter that. Enter your login name in the User ID box and your password in the Password box (your host will have provided you with both of these when you signed up). Remember to mask the password to make it appear in asterisks. In the Initial Remote Directory box enter the web server directory that your host provider assigned to you. In the Initial Local Directory enter the drive and directory on your computer where your files are stored. Click OK to save your settings.

- Once you have done this you are ready to upload files. You must first log on to the Internet. In the FTP Site Manager Dialogue box make sure that the site you have just added is highlighted. Click the Connect button. This will automatically connect you to your host provider. Click OK when a Login Message dialogue box appears. The window on the left should show your computer files and you web server files on the right. You host provider may have assigned a special directory for your files such /www, use this to put your files in. Highlight the files you want to upload on the left, select the Command menu and then select Upload. CuteFTP will send your files one by one to the Web server. You can now exit and go and look at your Web pages.

If you are going to sell your novel or manuscript from your own website you may have to consider using a secure payment facility so you can accept credit card payments. Your host may provide such facilities, along with shopping cart software. You will need to set up a Merchant bank account too. You could consider using **pay2see** (www.pay2see.com) who offer a number of services which enable you to sell electronic material over the internet. Pay2see deal with the credit card side of things and it only costs $99.00. **Clickbank** (www.clickbank.com) works in a similar way to pay2see and is cost effective if you are selling your own material.

Obviously before you can start selling the material on your website you will need to advertise the fact that you have a website. Attracting potential customers is one of the major problems on the internet; it is not impossible, it just takes a lot of dedication. First of all you must consider listing the URL of your site with as many search engines as you can find. You could start by using the ones we have listed in the handbook. Some of the search engines, such as Yahoo (www.yahoo.co.uk) have a business express service; for a fee of $199.00 (non-refundable) they will guarantee that one of their editors will look at your site within seven days. They don't guarantee inclusion in Yahoo but at least someone is looking at your page. Just make sure you include your website in the correct Yahoo category to begin with, it would be a shame to pay $199.00 and be put in the wrong place.

It can also help to exchange links with other likeminded writers, or to list your-self with as many writing related sites as you can find, if they will let you. Consider also using Usenet newsgroups, mailing lists, and of course, word of mouth.

Some more useful tips:

- Select and download a Web-page editor. Several simple editors are available for free; Netscape Composer is one. These editors let you see what your site will look like as you build it, so you won't have to learn HTML or other pro-gramming languages. Your Web-page editor will give you specific instruc-tions about options such as naming your site, creating different sections, creating backgrounds, adding links and inserting images.
- Remember that anyone with internet access can view your website; be care-ful about how much personal information you provide.
- Create images for your site by drawing them with your computer's paint pro-gram or by using a scanner for photographs and other hard-copy images.
- If you find an image on another Web page that you'd like to use, email the page's owner or administrator and request permission to download and post it. Download an image from a website by right-clicking on it (or clicking and holding on a Mac) and selecting Save Picture.
- Make sure your pages are compatible with both Netscape Navigator and Internet Explorer.

- Once you have created a Web page you like, you can use it as the basis for other pages. Simply choose Template and locate the Web page when creating a new page. So you might want to create a blank page with all the background elements for your site first, then use that as the basis for additional pages.

Where is it all going?

The internet provides many markets for writers and it seems every day there are new sites to consider. Although the handbook has looked at what can now be considered as the more 'traditional' web markets, there are always new possibilities opening up.

Sites such as Content Exchange, www.content-exchange.com, provide a facility for writers to display their work to a particular audience. There are three ways to accomplish this, you can create a free profile in their 'Talent Database', search their site for paying venues, or you can place an ad in their Classified Ad area describing the sort of work you are seeking, or post existing content. Although at the present time Content Exchange makes no charges for searching their databases this looks set to change. They are planning to charge a subscription fee at some point in the future although neither a pricing schedule or a time scale for this has been announced. They will continue to create and update profiles for no charge.

EPNworld (Internet Press Agency), is an umbrella organisation: http://www.correspondent.com and http://newsatsource.com are their two main services. Newsatsource.com gives buyers quick access to journalists on the ground and to stories that interest them, while journalists use correspondent.com to submit their work to the world's editors. Articles submitted to correspondent.com are posted on EPNworld's front page and listed in the searchable database. They are looking for writers with a proven track record and they check applicants for professional credentials before accepting them as members. You can sign up with them on site for no charge. Journalists set the price and copyright terms of articles they submit.

There are a number of sites where authors can post articles that can be read by any visitor to the site. **Themestream**, http://www.themestream.com, is one of these. Their topics are based on 'personal interest' categories, which have 1,500 topic areas. There are two types of 'personal interest' topics: 1) things that people love to do and 2) things that people need to track, such as finances, health, etc. You can submit articles that range from between 300 and 1,500 words, but if your article is longer you can break it up into two or three shorter pieces. Contributors make money based on the number of independent page views their articles receive. The rate per page view is 2 cents. Payment is made at the end of each calendar quarter. You retain copyright to your material, they only ask for non-exclusive rights to display your articles on their site or other sites. You can submit articles by clicking on the 'contribute' button on the left corner of 'MyThemes' page but you must select an appropriate topic area in which to post your article. If you can't find a suitable 'topic' you can suggest a new topic to their Librarian. You can change and modify material but you cannot delete it, although you can 'pull' your article so no one can see it. Themestream also operates a rating system, which allows them to decide which articles should stay 'active' and those that should be archived as new material comes online. The more ratings an article receives the more stars it receives. Four stars is the highest rating you can achieve, but if you receive no ratings they will put an 'NR' next to your name or article. But they have dramatically cut back on their list of topics over the past months.

Word Archive, http://www.wordarchive.com, in a similar fashion, pays the author based on the advertising revenue generated from their page. Each of your articles will contain advertising when they are viewed and you will receive 70% of any revenue earned through this advertising. They support two types of banner adverts. The first collects revenue on a 'per view' basis, i.e. on the number of times the advert is viewed. The second is based on 'per click' revenue, which is generated by a visitor clicking on an advert and going to the linked site. Obviously revenue is based on how many times adverts are viewed or clicked on the people visiting your work. Writers are paid by bankdrafts, which are sent out every twelve months or when your income exceeds $250.00. Anyone can open an 'account' but they will reject anything that is not good enough. They do allow you to put up your writing history, articles and a short bio so you can effectively present yourself as a package if that's what you want. Authors are actively encouraged to participate in the development of the site and asked to participate in referendums on policy.

About.com, http://www.about.com, is a similar type of site to Word Archive; but it employs 'Guides' to write material for them. They provide all the back up to enable this, but effectively you are just creating a website on a particular subject that will become part of the bigger picture. If you want to become a guide you will have to fill out an application form in the first instance, and then if you are accepted undertake a fairly rigorous virtual training course, called 'Orientation', which lasts for three weeks. Every applicant is assigned a 'personal mentor' to guide them through the Orientation period. Once you have 'graduated' (only 25% of all people who apply are accepted) you will be assigned an Editor who will provide feedback on topics, grammar, etc. They estimate that becoming a Guide requires at least 10-20 hours of work per week. All Guides share a portion of 30% of About.com's net ad revenues and they can stand to make a minimum of $100-500 a month, with a chance to make more. You own the copyright to all content and material you create in the feature and newsletter areas of your About site; they own other areas and you give them a license to use your material on the internet.

Instant Agora, http://www.instantagora.com/, they say, "is an interactive community where members can exchange ideas, experiences, opinions, and eventually items with other members from around the world." You earn points by posting messages in the member forums (1-5 pts), participating in surveys (10 pts), rating sites (25 pts), reviewing products and services (25 pts) and writing articles and opinions (50 pts) on subjects related to any of their categories. The points you earn can be exchanged for cash, and gift certificates, etc. Each point is worth 0.1c, but they may increase or decrease this figure. The site had not been officially launched at the time of writing, but it is an interesting concept and possibly writers should take a closer look when the site has been up and running for a few months.

Sites like **Rose Dog**, http://www.rosedog.com act as an online agent, allowing writers to submit work, which is displayed on the site and then promoted to publishers and other markets. If they sell any of your material they will take a percentage of the royalties. Their contract is not exclusive, allowing the author to pursue other avenues for their work and the search engine and work organiser on site helps agents and publishers evaluate manuscripts quickly. Their software tracks what agents and publishers have read and what their response is – so they can keep a manuscript under consideration, organise it into folders for later review and forward it to colleagues for comment and follow up. There is no fee for their services either to authors or agents and publishers. You can display a complete work or samples of your material and you can revise your work as often as you want. If an agent or publisher wants to contact you, they may do so through a messaging system, which also allows you to contact other writers or readers. Any personal information you submit to them is only available to those agents and publishers who have registered with the site. Your email address is kept confidential. All authors have an 'Account Statement' where they can keep track of how many people looked at their manuscript or how often their manuscript features in searches. All work is showcased in "plain text", which means any formatting will not show. Authors retain all rights to their material, Rosedog simply asks for permission to put the material in their showcase. You must become a member but this entitles you to post new work, update your current work, remove your work from the showcase, receive messages from agents, publishers and readers, and check interest in your work through your Account Statement.

GoodStory.com, www.GoodStory.com, which has recently been 'acquired' by Creative Planet, offers a platform for film scripts as well as plays, articles, short stories and books. Writers can post a short description of their book, short story, article, screenplay or even a full manuscript on the site. They advertise the service as 'a literary marketplace where writers can directly interact and connect with producers, publishers, agents and managers'. Everything is confidential and material can only be accessed with the writer's permission. At this stage it is only possible to register because they are still beta testing, but you can email them if you are interested in participating in the testing phase. During this phase the service is being offered at no charge. The site was supposed to go live in March 2000; hopefully by the time this book is published in February 2001 there will be some action!

The practice of internet rights trading is in its infancy, and probably best suited to publishers and agents, but there are a number of new sites that offer authors the chance to maximise their rights revenue, in a similar way to GoodStory.com. **Rightsworld.com**, www.rightsworld.com, is one such site. It is literally 'a twenty-four hour auction marketplace for the exchange of intellectual property in the publishing industry'. A seller, which could be an author, simply enters the terms of the contract, details of the auction and property, uploads the property and the bidding begins. They charge a listing fee of $19.95 per title not per right. When your property sells they charge a 5% commission fee. They have recently set up a strategic partnership with the National Writers Union (US), enabling their entire membership to trade rights. To get started you will need to open an account. Email: info@rightsworld.com, or visit their help centre to get more details.

These sites offer an opportunity to reach a wide market and secure an income and no doubt as the internet moves onto the next stage in its growth this new generation of sites will be overtaken by the next generation and so on. All the writer need do is keep informed and read the small print.

Where the e-book is going is another matter. When Gemstar announced that it had bought SoftBook Press and NuvoMedia and rolled their products into the neatly re-named Gemstar eBook the industry sat up and took notice. When it went on to announce that it had signed content agreements with five US publishers, the industry sat up ramrod straight. The deal releases six titles from a selection of best selling authors (including Patricia Cornwell, Robert Ludlum, James Patterson and Ken Follett) exclusively on the Gemstar eBook for a period of ninety days before the books are put into print. Publishers currently involved are Pearson-owned Penguin Putnam, Simon & Schuster, Warner Books, St Martin's Press and Harlequin (Mills & Boon). E-book readers will be able to download digital books using the modem installed in each Gemstar eBook and dial directly to a Gemstar server to buy these books.

Random House UK, in a weak attempt to play catch up announced early in 2000 that they were going to offer an electronic publishing programme. They gave no specific dates but suggested it would not be until 2001. Their list includes authors such as Roddy Doyle, Thomas Harris, Ben Elton and Irvine Welsh. Simon & Schuster have followed suit. Penguin and Faber's plans for an e-book list are also well in advance, and even Amazon has announced an e-book list. Taylor

& Francis, which includes the imprints Routledge, Falmer Press and UCL Press, have announced a digitisation programme in conjunction with Versaware, to be in place by the end of 2001. In fact, Taylor & Francis sent out a letter to its authors asking for their consent to digitise their books. Many UK publishers will no doubt replicate this move in the months to follow, because it is clear that most of them will need a list of e-books when the e-reader arrives in the UK.

Everything, however, still seems rather woolly, and although it is Random Houses' intention to create a distinct UK market, it becomes difficult to understand how they will accomplish this when you realise that each author's book will be available for download anywhere in the world. If they do not control the electronic rights world- wide and Random House US already have an e-list with the same authors on it then the UK operation will become increasingly marginalised.

There are also rumblings in the industry about the effects of Gemstar's pricing and marketing policies. Many feel it is an attempt to dictate how people will buy and read e-books. The price of their e-readers at $299 and $699 seems to fly in the face of the aim to make this technology available to the mass market. Gemstar has effectively abandoned the philosophy behind the Rocket eBook, if not the Rocket eBook itself, by adding a modem to its new devices allowing the sale of books to consumers by dialling up a catalogue on the web. They are also relying heavily on the bestseller, which is bad news for the writer who sees the internet as a new, open market for their work away from the traditional print based slog, and bad news for the customer who will find themselves locked into a catalogue of the tried and tested. If Gemstar are to lead the way, it means that many of the main players in e-reader technology will follow suit. It seems a shame that greed may upset a technology that was the first breath of fresh air the writer had had in years.

However, all is not lost. E-books abound on the internet, available in easily downloadable formats onto all sorts of hand-held devices, onto your computer and laptop. E-publishers are fiercely promoting the work of new and untried authors in an attempt to offer distinctive 'genres' that cut across the print-based standards. They offer wonderful royalties, and are more than capable of promoting and marketing their authors' work very effectively.

The future looks rosy. The technology is here to stay and although many people consider reading a book on an electronic device to be anathema, it will undoubtedly become a more realistic and attractive prospect as the devices become increasingly user friendly and less of a strain on the wallet. Both of these elements will be a reality sooner rather than later. Not all change is for the good, but the benefits must be recognised and there is simply no reason why people should not appreciate good literature, well written material or access to information, just because it is presented in a new form.

GLOSSARY OF TERMS

Adobe Acrobat - A book reading programme. It creates files that can be displayed on most platforms, and most e-publishers offer books for download in PDF because it is so versatile.

applet - Small software applications that allow data to be manipulated locally on the user's computer, decreasing the bandwidth needed to run networked programs.

ASCII - is an acronym for American Standard Code for Interface Interchange. It is a file format that contains no text formatting so it is transferable between different operating systems and programmes and is universally used for exchanging information between computers.

attach(ment) - An attachment facility allows you to 'attach' one or several files (usually indicated by a paperclip) to your email.

authoring - The process of creating a title for distribution.

banner adverts - The internet's version of a billboard, usually found on the top of a search engine or a website. It is usually a rectangular box at the top of the page through which to click to another site.

Berne Convention - Outlines internet copyright laws.

bitmap - A way of representing images for the computer. It is essentially the pattern of dots that make up a picture and can be manipulated by a computer.

Boolean logic (AND, OR, NOT, NEAR) - AltaVista and Excite use Boolean, or proximity, operators (always in uppercase) instead of includes and excludes (+/).

bookmark - A way to list a favourite website that is retained in the browser's bookmark menu for retrieval at a later date.

browser - A computer programme used to navigate the WWW and display its content.

chat room - 'rooms' where you can meet and talk online by posting comments onto the screen for others to read.

CD-ROM - Any compact disk with data on it. The term CD-ROM usually means a non-audio disk. These days CD-ROM is used in reference to disks containing data that can be used in a computer system.

CD-ROM drive - A device that reads data from CD-ROM disks into a computer.

Clear Type - A computer screen consists of thousands of small dots, pixels, which compose the picture. Clear Type can make each pixel display more than one colour, so they are less 'blocky', and the smoother image is easier to read.

ClickBank - A secure payment service.

compact disk - A plastic disk with a reflective surface on one side that can be encoded and read with a laser beam.

compression - A technique for reducing the amount of data needed to store digital information.

contract period - The contract period signifies how long the contract will be binding once you have signed it.

copyright - is 'the legal exclusive right of the author of a creative work to control the copying of that work'.

cursor - A movable pointer symbol on the computer screen used to locate the current screen position of the user. Can indicate a choice or access a hyperlink.

domain name - A particular name chosen by you for your website. Normally a fee is paid annually for a domain name.

database - A library of related information, which can accessed electronically through a computer.

digital - In a form capable of being processed by a computer. Data converted to ones and zeros – the only type of information a computer is capable of processing.

dpi - Stands for 'dots per inch', a unit used to measure the resolution of a printer. The more dots per inch the sharper the image appears.

drag and drop - The process of selecting an object, either text or graphic, moving it to another location on the screen, and then releasing it onto another object for any type of processing or re-grouping.

drop-down field - An input field in which a pre-existing list of possible selections drops down when the user points to it with the cursor. The user then selects an item from the list.

e-author - An electronically published author.

e-book - Any form of electronic book in which contents are stored and played back digitally.

e-book reader - A software program that allows you to read an e-book downloaded from the internet.

e-cash - An electronic form of money – stored on your computers hard drive.

e-commerce - Business conducted solely on the internet

e-reader - An electronic hand held device for reading and downloading e-books.

encoding - Converting information to a digital format capable of being used by a particular system.

electronic rights - The right to publish your work on the internet. Electronic rights are owned by the author.

e-publisher - A publisher who publishes work on the internet to be downloaded from their web-site by interested parties. They do not publish work in print form.

ezine - An electronic magazine using much the same format as prints based magazines delivered via email.

FAQ - Frequently Asked Questions - a file containing background information on a topic.

floppy disk - A magnetic disk that can store date and can be removed and transported to another computer that uses the same operating system.

forum - Mailing list where you can participate in discussions about a particular topic, usually moderated some times not.

freespace - Space made available, either by an ISP or a search engine, to people who use their email facilities enabling them to create a website for no cost.

GIF - (Graphic Interchange Format) Web graphic formats.

Grant of rights - Electronic rights giving the e-publisher the right to publish an authors e-book in electronic form.

GLOSSARY OF TERMS

guidelines - A series of requirements to follow when submitting work to a website or an ezine – each publication or site will have their own guidelines.

FTP - File Transfer Protocol - an original internet protocol used to transfer data files in a non-interactive fashion.

home page - The first and main document that appears on a website, often directing the user to other pages.

host - A main computer used to control communications.

hot spot - A place on the screen (word, phase, and graphic) that contains a hyperlink. The hot spot can be linked to text elsewhere or it can trigger playback of an audio or video clip.

HTML - Hypertext Mark-up Language – the language used to code text files, primarily used for documents found on the web.

HTTP - yperText Transfer Protocol – An international standard transmission protocol used for web files.

hyperlink - A link between two related points in a database. The user can point with a cursor to one link and by pressing a button while the cursor is positioned over the first link, access the second link.

hypermedia - Multimedia that is interconnected by hyperlinks.

hypertext - Text that uses links to connect to other, often elaborating text.

JPEG - (Joint Photographic Experts Group) Web graphic format.

interactive - Media that responds to the user. Interactive media are connected via a system of links. They respond when the user points a cursor and clicks on them.

interactive fiction - Fiction that is created online.

internet - A series of interconnected networks with local, regional and national networks, using the same telecommunications protocol (TCP/IP). Provides email, remote login and file transfer. The web is communicated via the internet.

internet2 - Internet2 will enable applications, such as tele-medicine, digital libraries and virtual laboratories that are not possible within today's internet technology. It will not replace the internet as we know but rather enhance its original capabilities.

internet Address - A unique numeric address that identifies a computer connected to the internet.

Intranet - A Computer network that is used for internal internet communication.

Java - A programming language developed and promoted by Sun Microsystems for sending programs called 'applets' over the internet. These applets are sent in partially compiled form and are then fully compiled by the user's computer.

keywords - selected words used to define a search.

link - A hypertext path connecting one part of a document to other documents.

mailing list - Sends an individual copy of a message to a subscriber usually arriving as an email.

manuscript format - In what form a particular ezine or web-site wishes to receive manuscripts. Double spaced, etc.

menu - A text or graphic screen that lists choices for users, which can be selected by pointing with the cursor and clicking.

message board - an online message board where you can post comments, and ask questions. Other people can read your message, respond or leave their own message.

Microsoft Reader - The Microsoft Reader is an e-book-reading program available for PC's.

moderate - A system used to control the content of postings on newsgroups, or used to 'police' a chat room. These moderated groups are usually controlled by the presence of a 'moderator' who makes sure everyone behaves themselves.

multimedia - A medium which combines text, audio and video in an interactive product or service.

multiple submissions - Submitting more than one manuscript to the same publisher.

new media - Any electronic media employing interactive means for its expression.

news groups - A world wide distributed bulletin board system allowing internet users around the world to submit messages to certain newsgroups; these messages are delivered to every internet hosts that wants them.

online - A service which provides access to a database over telephone lines such as when connecting to the internet.

Open eBook Forum - The OeBF has launched a standards co-ordination initiative to bring together developments in e-book and e-publishing platforms.

operators - Operators are symbols or special words that sit alongside the keywords in a query and tell the search engine how to process them. These can be used to refine searches. Operators let users specify whole phrases or words to exclude, or words that should appear, and words that should appear close together.

page counter - A page counter measures how many people visit a web-site.

Pay2see - A secure payment service.

PDA 'personal digital assistant', such as a Palm Pilot.

Phrase searching - A system by which it is possible to specify phrases by putting them in quotation marks ("") when conducting a search on the internet.

portal sites - Provide an opening page to a web browser that can be tailored to individual needs.

posting - Putting a message on a newsgroup or submitting details about yourself to an ezine or job market.

Printing on demand (POD) - A book is prepared up to the stage when it is ready for printing. Printing will not take place until an order to purchase a copy is actually received.

royalties - Royalties are an agreed percentage paid to the author on the sale of each e-book.

RTF - Microsoft's Rich Text File. Rich Text Format (RTF) saves all formatting. Converts formatting to instructions that other programmes can read and interpret.

search engine - The computer program that allows the location and retrieval of information in a database, such as Yahoo UK.

secure server - Allows for secure payments to be made by credit card over the internet.

server - A computer connected to a network and used to provide services such as a web page or directing email.

GLOSSARY OF TERMS

simultaneous submission - Submitting a manuscript to more than one market at a time.

snail mail - Mail sent by post as opposed to email.

spamming - A technique used by many companies to advertise their products via email, usually done anonymously and in large numbers.

submission guidelines - A list of requirements needed when submitting a manuscript to a particular online magazine, ezine or website.

tag - Any of many code strings embedded in an HTML document which determine graphical layout, hyperlinks, and embedded objects such as Java written applets or multimedia file downloading and opening.

termination - Every contract should have a termination clause that protects both the publisher and the author by setting a date upon which either party can terminate the contract.

text only - Saves text without any formatting.

TCP/IP - A set of protocol that standardise data transfer between computers connected to the internet

title - An electronic work, for either CD-ROM or online distribution that employs new media

tree-fiction - A type of online interactive novel developed on the internet. Allows the reader to control how the story will develop.

URL - Uniform Resource Locator – an address describing a specific document on the Web.

USENET - A large number of globally available newsgroups in which users may post and read messages.

user - The person who navigates the web or uses a software program.

VDU - Visual display unit – the screen.

web browservA software program used to access the web and use hyperlinks to more from site to site, such as Netscape of Internet Explorer. Also used in conjunction with software plug-in programs to listen to audio files, view video programs.

Web-page editor - Text editors create HTML code and allow you to view your site as you build it.

web server - A computer holding web pages and used to distribute them over a network.

website - A collection of inter-linked files and documents written with HTML and available on the internet.

Windows - A user-friendly operating system used in most computers with Intel-made CPU's.

World Wide Web - WWW – The worldwide network of computers and documents that uses HTML mark-up language.

INDEX

A
About.com, 266
Adobe Acrobat, 132, 271
Alta Vista, 238, 239
ASCII, 19, 271
Association of Authors' Agents, The, 233
attach(ment), 17, 19, 271

B
basic guidelines, 15
BBC Webguide, 252
Beaucoup, 252
Berne Convention, 271
Boolean logic, 236, 271

C
chat rooms, 14, 272, 277
checklist, e-publishing sites, 139
Clear Type, 272
ClickBank, 262, 272
Cnet Builder.com, 260
Content Exchange, 264
Competitions, 257-9
Content providers, 11
Contract, 227, 230
contract period, 228, 272
contract, sample, 230
copyright, 18, 226, 227, 228, 231, 272
costs, 136, 228
creative control, 229

CuteFTP, 261
CuteHTML, 261
Cybook, The, 134

D
defining, search, 235
digital rights, management (DRM), 136
Domain Valet, 261
dpi, 21, 273

E
e-book, 9, 130-140, 227-229, 273, 274, 277
e-book reader, 130-131, 273
e-books, 130-138, 152, 260, 274
e-book rights, 233
electronic magazine, 10
Electronic Newstand, 252
electronic publications, 10-129
electronic publishing, 58, 130, 255, 268
electronic rights, 227, 228, 233, 274
EPNworld, 264
e-publisher, 130, 227-229, 271, 274
e-publishers, A-Z, 142-219
e-publishing, 137, 140, 141, 228, 229, 277
excludes, 236
ezine, 10-12, 14-17
ezines, A-Z listing, 23-129

F
fanzine, 10
FAQ, 12, 274
finding markets, 16
fiction, writing, 40, 94
file size, 20

File Transfer Protocol, 261
format, 18-20, 130, 274-276
Forum One, 253
FTP, 241, 261, 262, 275

G
Gemstar, 268, 269
Gemstar eBook, 132, 268
genre, sites, 11-12
GIF, 17, 274
Glassbook, 132, 144
GoReader, 135
GoodStory.com, 267, 268
grant of rights, 228, 231, 274
Graphic Images, 18
GraphX, 18
Guidelines, 15, 17, 275

H
Host provider, 261, 262
HMTL Writers Guild, 260
HTML, 19, 20, 260, 261, 263, 275, 280

I
includes, 236
Infoseek, 234, 236, 244, 248, 275
interactive, 14, 275
Internet Explorer, 19, 280
Internet Public Library, The, 252
ISP, 244, 274

J
JPEG, 17, 275

K
keywords, 235, 236, 249, 251, 252, 276
Korea eBook, 134

L
links, 13, 14, 276
literary ezines, 10, 102
Lview Pro, 18
Lycos, 234, 245

M
mail, snail, 279
manuscript format, 276
marketing, 140, 269
markets, 12, 15-17
market research, 15
Microsoft Reader, 131, 134, 154, 185, 204, 277
multiple submissions, 21, 277

N
Netscape Navigator, browser, 19, 263
newsletter, 10
non-fiction, writing, 15

O
online magazines, A-Z listing, 10-129
online, e-publishers, A-Z listing, 142, 219
online publishing, 142-219
online resources, 254-256
Open eBook Forum, 135, 277
Operators, 235-237, 250, 271, 277

P
Paint Shop Pro, 18

pay2see, 262, 278
payment, 11, 12, 231
payment, royalty, 220
PDA, 130, 278
phrase searching, 236, 278
POD, 278
poetry, websites, 16, 32, 36, 47, 55, 71, 73, 80, 86, 98, 104, 105, 109, 125, 258
promotion, 228, 229
Publishers Association, The, 233
publishers, online, 142-219

Q
Quick reference, ezines, 113-119
Quick guide, royalty payments, 220-225

R
research, 258
resolution, 21
resources, online, 14, 21, 22, 254-256
rich text, 19
rights, 18
Rightsworld.com, 268
Rocket eBook, 132, 133
Rose Dog, 266
royalties, 137, 140, 227, 229, 233, 267, 278
royalty payments, 220-225
RTF, 19, 278

S
Sales, 229
search engines, 234-236, 238-253, 278
search methods, 234
simulataneous submissions, 21, 279
snail mail, 279

Society of Authors, 227, 233
Softbook, 132, 154, 195, 213, 214, 268
statistics, web site, 11, 90, 148, 234
submission procedures, 17, 19, 257, 258
submitting work, 20, 72, 275

T
technical terms, 17-21
termination, contract, 229, 279
Themestream, 265
text editors, 280

U
URL, 11, 241, 249, 262, 263, 279
useful tips, search methods, 263
useful tips, website assessment, 13

V
Vanity publishers, 137

W
web browser, 242, 278, 280
Web crawlers, search engines, 240, 250
Web Monkey, 260
Web-page editor, 247, 261, 264
web server, 261, 262, 280
website assessment, 13, 14
website, creating a, 260, 266
webzines, 10
Word Archive, 265, 266
Writer's Digest, 21, 259
Writer's Write, 22
writing for the web, 10, 14-16, 99
WritingNow.com, 21

WSTP, 261
WWW, 280

Y
Yahoo, 234, 251, 261, 263

Z
Zine, 10